Laura Coffey's personal Odyssey is a magical and hugely captivating journey into journeys. Like the original Odyssey and all that follow it, *Enchanted Islands* is about finding one's way home. But the adventures on the way are filled with such beauty, wonder and surprise. The journey changes the meaning of the destination. A simply marvellous read, hugely recommended.

Stephen Fry

If you love memoir and Greek mythology (as I do) this is a delight. Coffey escapes a grim and lonely pandemic for volcanos and orange-blossom brioche, kingfishers and tales of Circe. But life lies ready to sting, like the Medusa jellyfish she encounters on her evening swims. A spellbinding book about growing up, grieving and the gods.

Clare Pollard, author of *Delphi*

The Odyssey is the perfect guide for this bold and personal, honest and witty journey of reflection and discovery, grief and recovery.

Michael Scott, Professor of Classics & Ancient History at the University of Warwick

Numinous – like Cezanne's oranges, this is full of the magic of daily realities. A journey that proposes a way to navigate between the sadness and joy of our complex lives.

Maria Balshaw, CEO Tate Galleries

Enchanted Islands beautifully captures the places where the distant past pushes up against the immediate present. Coffey takes us with her on a sensory tour of the islands of the Mediterranean, enhanced by charming inclusions of mythology and history. You can feel the cool of the October sea and taste the bittersweet burn of well-sugared espresso. Coffey's skill as a travel guide does not end there, however. The inclusion of her father's end-of-life experience elevates and centers the story, taking the reader on an exploration of that most mysterious of countries – grief.

Luna McNamara, author of *Psyche and Eros*

I raced through this book, heart hammering, in a single sitting. It's about a death, and about the pandemic, love and loss and yearning. But as much, if not more, it's a book about the joyful, agonising, complicated business of being alive. The words sing of sun on the skin, of cold water and ripe fruit. The ideas are profound, the language exquisite.

Marianne Levy, author of *Don't Forget to Scream*

I read Laura's journey in a single day. An intimately shared voyage of grief and hope – stunning!

Freya Bromley, author of *The Tidal Year*

Enchanted Islands is beautifully written, moving and heartfelt, but also funny: sharply observed travel-writing cleverly interwoven with memoir and myth. Laura Coffey writes with sensuous vividness about Mediterranean islands, Homer's *Odyssey* and her father's illness and death. If you loved *H is For Hawk* or *Grief is the Thing with Feathers*, this book is for you.

**Nick Higham, author and former presenter,
Meet the Author, BBC News**

Lovelorn and escaping lockdown, Laura finds solace in her bridge between myths and science, the melding of maps and poetry, and the healing power of the natural world. Weaving joy and heartbreak, this bittersweet, lyrical memoir is a truly moving odyssey – it will make you yearn to jump on a ship and let the winds pull you away...

Beth Morrey, *Sunday Times* bestselling author

Sparkling and changing like the sea in all its shades of darkness and light, Laura's beautifully written odyssey is about embracing your freedom, becoming the goddess and enchanting yourself, weaving and unweaving your story. It gently reminds us that in life, we don't get to choose the route, but we can find islands of enchantment.

Jennifer Barclay, author of *An Octopus in My Ouzo*

This is travel writing at its finest. Local colour, history, memoir, and an emotional journey through grief and joy weave together beautifully. It is literary without pretension, informative while entertaining, moving and heartfelt while also being sharply funny. The best travel writing inspires us to journey ourselves, and this book made me long for warm Mediterranean islands. A triumph of a first book from an enchanting author.

Noah Charney, bestselling author and BBC presenter

Enchanted Islands deftly combines memoir, escapist travelogue, and meditations on the Greek classics. It's also wryly funny and deserves to be widely read by travellers and lovers alike.

James Crabtree, author of *The Billionaire Raj* and former *Financial Times* journalist

So engrossing – I was right there with Laura on her travels and in her grief. *Enchanted Islands* is mesmerising and moving, a feast for the senses and the soul.

Joanne Mallon, career coach and author of *Change Your Life in 5 Minutes a Day*

Enchanted Islands

An Hachette UK Company
www.hachette.co.uk

Summersdale Publishers
Part of Octopus Publishing Group Limited
Carmelite House
50 Victoria Embankment
LONDON
EC4Y 0DZ
UK

www.summersdale.com

This FSC® label means that materials used for the product have been responsibly sourced

FSC
www.fsc.org
MIX
Paper | Supporting responsible forestry
FSC® C104740

Printed and bound by Clays Ltd, Suffolk, NR35 1ED

ISBN: 978-1-83799-313-0

Substantial discounts on bulk quantities of Summersdale books are available to corporations, professional associations and other organizations. For details contact general enquiries: telephone: +44 (0) 1243 771107 or email: enquiries@summersdale.com.

Enchanted Islands

TRAVELS THROUGH MYTH & MAGIC, LOVE & LOSS

Laura Coffey

summersdale

For Theo

Contents

The events in this book are true, although occasionally I've played around with timelines and locations, and have, now and then, collapsed complexity for narrative purposes. For example, I have two brothers and use 'my brother' as shorthand.

Some people who appear in the book have been disguised to protect their identities – names and appearances have been changed – and I've created some composite characters, like the boyfriend who is not one single person but represents a combination of people I've dated. The breakup described is, similarly, a composite of my experiences. Other people have been generous enough to let me use their real names and tell their stories.

Travel was in line with the different countries' entry criteria, which was set by their respective governments' assessment of risk at the time. I was lucky to be able to travel and acutely aware of the privilege and of the risks both to myself and others. I did my best to mitigate these, by following the regulations of the places I visited, and observing local guidance.

Almost everything described in the book happened outside, including meals. People wore masks, applied hand gel, kept distance. I haven't written a lot about the pandemic in the text, or listed all these precautions every time, because it can be tedious to keep reading the same points. Instead, please be aware that this forms the backdrop to the story.

For more, see the Afterword at the end of the book.

'to find in motion what was lost in space'

Tennessee Williams

'You think about bathing in the sea – thick as velvet, supple and smooth as a wild animal. You think about swimming naked, and at night, with the stars, and a friend. Swim till you're far from the world, and breathing together in the same rhythm, and free of absolutely everything.'

Albert Camus

EUROPE

FRANCE

SPAIN

Menorca
*Island of
the Cyclops*

ALGERIA

TUNISIA

NORTH AFRICA

CROATIA

ITALY

Korčula
Calypso's
Island

Mljet

Sicily

Island of
the Sun God

Egadi
Archipelago

Marettimo
Sunny Ithaca

↓

↑

Favignana
*Island full
of wonders*

° Trapani

Sicily

Aẽolian Archipelago ~

Stromboli

Island of Aeolus, guardian of the winds

Salina

Lipari

Vulcano

milazzo

Island of the Sun God, the god of human joy

Chapter One

Find the Beginning

London, England

Tell me about a complicated man.
Muse, tell me how he wandered and was lost
when he had wrecked the holy town of Troy,
and where he went, and who he met, the pain
he suffered on the sea, and how he worked
to save his life and bring his men back home.
He failed, and for their own mistakes, they died.
They ate the Sun God's cattle, and the god
kept them from home. Now, goddess, child of Zeus,
tell the old story for our modern times.
Find the beginning.

The Poet to the Muse

It started with a boy, like it always does. Otherwise I probably wouldn't have left London and would never have bothered picking up a copy of *The Odyssey*. He had a triple-first in English literature from a prestigious university, and I was trying to impress him. Later, when I think back, I'll remember that his degree class was one of the triple-first things he ever told me, and this should have been a warning. That somehow, despite it being awarded more than two decades ago, it was still important for him to tell me just how clever he was, the exact strata he occupied. But at this point it was early days, I was under the old kind of enchantment and suspending disbelief. It probably helped that he was an amazing chef, that he was cooking me dinner, and that I was very hungry.

Emily Wilson would have no truck with this kind of pretension. She's a professor at the University of Pennsylvania and her new translation of *The Odyssey* has been met with much acclaim for its muscularity. It's the first English translation by a woman, and her version strips out the overwrought insertions of self-important nineteenth-century male poets, to make the language shine, plain and simple and clear. Her aim was to bring back the original musicality to the poem, to restore its pace and rhythms, to give it edge and tension. I was browsing in a bookshop a couple of months after that first dinner when I saw Emily's translation glittering with gold inlay on a table display and picked it up on a whim, exactly the way people arranging those table displays trick you into doing. I guess I was thinking I could attempt to catch up with him, or at least that reading it might give me something interesting to say about a discipline I was entirely ignorant about, or maybe it was simply a way of seeking more connection, but when I lifted it, the book was off-puttingly thick. I asked the bookseller if it was even readable. Her face lit up, 'It's wonderful,' she said, 'just get it.' I trusted this woman's judgement, she'd guided me to some particularly brilliant and strange and peculiar books previously. So I bought the book and it sat heavy in my bag. Back home when I opened it up, I saw the actual poem was pretty skinny, which was reassuring. He was probably clever enough to read the original Greek, but surely I could manage a translation. I added it to the stack of unread books on my bedside table where it stayed forgotten, for a while.

On one of our early dates I invited him to swim with me in Hampstead Ponds. He raised an eyebrow at the folly of the English, but he came and it was extremely cold and he pretended not to hate it, and I pretended not to know he hated it. He swam with me again, and again. Trying to like it with that determined, American kind of enthusiasm.

I had surgery – a dentist had broken something inside my face when he took out a wisdom tooth and there was infection and pain and a long emergency operation under general anaesthetic. When I came out of the hospital my face was bruised right down my neck to my collarbones and everything was swollen and there were stitches like spiders across the insides of my cheek. He gently tilted the angle of my jaw, slid his hand into my hair, touched my face so softly, the lightest pressure.

'You know I like spending time with you,' he said.

'No, I don't know,' I said, wanting reassurance.

'Come on – I swam in a freezing pond for you,' he said.

'What do you like about me?'

'How soft your skin is,' he skimmed it like a stone across water, 'your mouth.'

Six months later we were walking his dog along an abandoned railway route through North London. It wound through a nature reserve and everything was dark green and in bud. Birds rustled in the trees next to the path. The city was in transition, not sure of itself, we were expecting a curfew, we were not sure what to expect. It was hard to find somewhere to get coffee – the shops had started shutting ahead of official government guidance which was muddled and confused, but the sky was wide and open, the air was spring crisp and cold, and there was optimism amongst all the unease. I was wearing a bright blue coat and sunglasses and it made me feel better, less anxious, just being in motion, walking alongside him, having a destination to aim towards. He left the path to go and pee in the woods and as he came back he looked beautiful and I had this transitory surge of feeling for a moment in the cold spring sunshine. Something piercing.

In a supermarket, we shopped between the gaps: weird, panicky shortages – no soap, no loo roll. He was swapping eggs between two cartons so he got all the largest ones, something that it would never even have occurred to me to do in a million years. Except that he fumbled, smash-dropped two and turned red as the shop assistant walked over with the yellow Caution Wet Floor sign. I laughed at his embarrassment although to me this definitely felt like a step too far. The most I would ever do with eggs was flip the lid to check for breakages before putting them in my basket, and most of the time I barely remembered to even do that much.

Back in his mews house we cooked for hours. I liked the small scale of it, the domesticity. The dog and I already felt like family. I was chopping garlic but there was something I wasn't doing quite right and I was demoted to opening the wine. I admired his culinary precision, his insistence on methodical process, lacking nearly all discipline myself. How soothing, to chop and stir and taste and season when everything outside was in flux. I felt like an almost-wife although it had only been six months.

We ate and watched the news which was inconclusive. Then he reached for me. Slow kisses.

'I want everything.'

'Yeah?' He moved down.

'Is this good?'

'Yes, is it good for you?'

Afterwards I put my hand on his chest and he held it in place with both of his as he fell asleep.

The next morning I shapeshifted. I didn't want to get in his way while he worked from home, I really didn't want him to ask me to leave, so I went invisible or at least attempted semi-transparency. His work seemed to involve endless conference calls for the private equity fund he worked for. I wasn't working at all, because I'd just left my job with spectacularly bad timing. I had vague ideas about taking a break, going hiking in Chile, resetting before finding a new one. This would, of course, turn out to be one of the worst plans I'd ever thought of but for now the future wasn't clear.

I sat outside in the sun in a hammock in his garden, wrapped in a blanket under the froth of the pink apple tree. Occasionally, petals dropped, confetti-ing my hair like a bride. I was reading Emily's introduction to *The Odyssey* and watching him through the glass doors as I learned just how much disagreement there is about who the author was – probably, it wasn't written by a single 'Homer' but rather created by a bunch of people. Even when the poem was written is a matter of much debate. The best the quarrelling scholars can agree to is that it was written sometime between the late eighth and late seventh century BCE, which doesn't narrow it down all that much.

We remained cocooned in liminal time-space during the first spring warmth, while around us the city stilled and started sliding towards lockdown. The days looped and repeated. Waiting up late for the news drinking wine. Then those slow kisses, his hands in my hair and afterwards we slept, curled into each other. Time folded and concertinaed: a weekend became a week. Eventually, I thought I should go back across town to check on my flat. Before I left, I said fast, from uncertainty: 'Do you want to hang out more?'

'Yeah.' His answer came fast with a child's enthusiasm, then qualified, 'I mean there's nothing else to do.'

'Charming.'

'No. I didn't mean it like that. I meant I have no other plans.'

'Even more charming,' but I was smiling as I cycled back across the empty city.

I was sitting in the shared courtyard behind my flat with *The Odyssey* and a cup of coffee. The weather was beaming down at us – it was a remarkable spring despite the growing darkness in the world. No one could remember a prettier one, everyone was thankful for this fortunate weather, and confirming it with each other from a distance: aren't we lucky? These were the conversational beats we repeated with various combinations of neighbours, like dialogue in a badly improvised play.

In another section of her elegant introduction, Emily was explaining that Homer's poem 'has little interest in the realistic depiction of geography' and she was pretty dismissive of the scholars and readers across the ages who had attempted to map the fantastical story world onto the literal geography of the real world, but I quite liked this idea. To me there was something compelling about attempting to ground myths and mysticism, a twist of poetry in trying to nail the unreal down onto the real. I spent time looking at the hand-drawn maps that Emily included. The picture of the story world was laid out next to the actual cartography of the modern-day world, and I flicked repeatedly between them. I liked reading the competing theories of the scholars of the past who fought over which of the islands in the story might represent real-life Sicily, which of the modern-day Aeolian islets off the Italian coast could be the inspiration for the floating island home of Aeolus, the guardian of the winds. I looked up where Calypso's island might be plotted on the map. This is where Odysseus gets trapped for seven long, sexy years, forced into having an affair with a hot goddess. Theories abound and the story islands shifted and moved, skittering across the seas depending on whom you consulted. People claimed they were located everywhere from around modern-day Greece to far-flung islands across the other side of the Mediterranean Sea, even parts of the north coast of Africa. Mapping section completed, I started reading the actual poem, and it wasn't as annoying as you might think.

I was intermittently turning my phone over to check for messages and still there was nothing. It remained darkly silent. So much of dating is waiting, just like those fairy girls, the ones in the original tales, not the feminist revisions. Waiting, feigning indifference, adopting the passive tense, hoping the prince isn't going to be too much of a dick. A deeper, more intimate silence enveloped me, was suspended inside the quiet suspension of the world. A Russian doll of silences. The smallest one was a long-held pause: it had been more than a week since I left on my bicycle, and he hadn't even checked that I had made it back across town safely. There were no messages.

During this silent week I did what any sane girl would do and formulated a list of conspiracy theories, hypotheses and wild assumptions to test with my best friend, Rachel. Over many days I endlessly mapped imagined possibilities, became a professor of cartography, charting, measuring. I forensically replayed conversations and performed keyhole surgical analysis, with Rachel handing me the necessary instruments. Together we tested and probed and cauterised, and found nothing that explained anything. It wasn't as if he could be too busy, there was literally nothing to do. Everything had stopped moving and gone deadly still. Static crackled. Eventually the silence became too loud and full and anxious for me to bear. I've never been much good at playing it cool. So I asked, and when he answered it all clicked together, and it wasn't what I expected.

I wrote to him: *You're very quiet – everything okay?*

The reasons, of course, were boring and clichéd, like they always are. There was someone else that he was emotionally involved with, she lived abroad, he wasn't sure if she felt the same way, he wanted to find out.

I stopped reading and pictured her. An offshore girlfriend. Tanned legs. Smooth, tax-efficient movements, walking along the shoreline, picking up shells. It had been half a year, all the rhythms of romance: dinners, movies, trips away, flowers (mostly ones I bought him in reverse feminist enthusiasm), a valentine's card I'd handmade, designed to make him laugh.

A second text pinged, graciously offering to continue to 'hang out', in the meantime. He ended with the symbol for a kiss. Or crossbones.

After all that, it turned out to be just another boring variation on the classics. Once upon a time, in a country far, far away, true love was locked in a tower. Part of her allure, no doubt. Newly shipwrecked in high pandemic waves, I channelled Emily Wilson, and wrote a translation, sending my revised version to Rachel:

Dear Candidate,

We regret to inform you that the position of New Girlfriend with benefits package 'Romance' is taken. We have sourced a perfect global candidate with precisely the right skill set that we're now in the process of on-shoring. We apologise for any misunderstanding on your part. Perhaps we were not quite as clear as we could have been over the six-month interview process – with team-building challenges and take-home assignments, that all along we had an alternative candidate in mind, with whom we felt a deep emotional connection. However, we have an exciting new opportunity for Interim Girlfriend with the job title Mistress. This is short-term pre-maternity cover, until New Girlfriend is relocated. The role is a lesser grade, and we recognise it's not the position you interviewed for. Of course, the benefits package is slightly different. There is no long-term incentive plan element (for obvious reasons!) and the duties are tactical rather than strategic. We'd like you to take the position although if you decide not to then we're kind of indifferent. We're just trying to be honest and straightforward post-hoc. We hope you appreciate that's a big gesture on our part. We're being quite sensitive and emotionally intelligent (if not emotionally available!) and we congratulate ourselves on being so awesome. It took a lot for us to admit that the position was taken and we are not going to feel bad about it. If you reject our kind offer we reserve the right to label your response bitter and tell our friends how 'psycho' you are. It's probably all your fault for not realising since we gave you some pretty damn clear signals. Actually, we're kind of angry with you about the whole thing tbh. We are starting to question *your* competence. Maybe *you* should think about that.

Rachel called me laughing. She was finally pregnant after trying forever, so even if it was legal to see her, I couldn't put her at any risk. These were the early days when we weren't sure about what was spreading the virus, and were all paranoid we might be accidentally killing people just by going to the supermarket. I realised this as I talked to her, holding my phone to my ear in the hushed city, that now I couldn't just nip over to see her and feel better, and I remembered how newly alone I was. More bad timing, this stupid ending just before something horrible was really beginning, just as the first brutal UK lockdown started up. He had omitted this information for so long already, couldn't he have kept it from me for longer so we could have kept each other company during the apocalypse?

I was living alone and immediately isolated, the perfect conditions to dwell and obsess, to pick over textual analysis, for blame to be introjected and metabolised. I'm also pretty smart so where had I missed the symbols and the subtext? Unsolvable equations: why would he want some semi-mythical figure who lived abroad when I was a real girl living in the same city and the world was in meltdown? Why wouldn't he at least have mentioned her before? Why weren't men routinely called manipulative but women were? What else had

I deliberately overlooked in order to be fully complicit in my own deception?

Heightened by world hysteria, my emotions felt less trustworthy than usual. It really had not been very long, there were no promises, although there was a fairly frank conversation about not wasting time. Maybe I'd made it all up in my head, seen tigers in shadows, skipped casual dating into a relationship. How stupid of me to think it was going somewhere, to have built in love and romance and a future. Deluded. Overreacting. It was far too early for it to be heartbreak. I wasn't falling in love, I'd just really liked him. But it was real. I was falling, it hadn't felt casual, I'd told him I was only interested in something serious, he'd made me feel he was in the same place, we'd talked about the future. He'd come swimming. He'd come to the hospital. He was wrong, not me. Why was I doubting myself, letting him reframe, tell me it was different to how it actually was, why was I abandoning myself, adopting his version of the truth? There was a connection between us, I could feel it. It had felt exciting and soft and lovely. It had felt real. I was sad and angry and confused and the weight of each kept changing and my thoughts kept circle-spinning and he never replied to the last text and he turned into a ghost and I was spinning and dizzy and couldn't stop spinning.

I knew it should have felt more like a grey disappointment, just sharpened by a lost chance to couple up with intensity as the world went flat, but if I'm honest, I wrote privately in my journal, it *is* kind of heartbreaking in that annoying *almost* or *unrealised potential* kind of way. That's the thing with heartbreak, it's not rational, it doesn't pay attention to timelines or data points, it just feels. I felt like I was splintering. I was swimming in Homer's 'wine-dark sea' and my head ached with it all. I crawled exhausted, dragging myself on to the shore, into my cave and lay staring up at the ceiling, sorely in need of grey-eyed, gold-shod Athena, Aeolus who rules the winds, all of the trickster gods, to be spun into their drama. To become enchanted.

As the real world became stranger and more terrifying with new monsters and perils, I dived deeper into the fantastical world of *The Odyssey*, in search of escape.

I kept reading the poem. I even read the footnotes.

'Find the beginning' instructs the Poet to the Muse as *The Odyssey* opens. The start is rarely where you think it should be. Often you can't figure out the actual beginning until much later, when you're almost at the end.

The Odyssey begins in the middle and declares up front that it's all about a 'complicated man'. He is deceitful and manipulative – but he's also very clever – and these traits endear him to Athena, who makes him one of her pets. Odysseus is trying to get home after the Trojan war, back to an island called Ithaca. He's longing to see his wife, Penelope, who's wise and enigmatic, and his son, who was just a baby when he left and is now a young man. But he has badly annoyed the vengeful gods in various ways, so they prevent his return and skip-skim his ship, sending it scuttering all over the place, far and wide across the sea. Odysseus has basically been island-hopping for an extremely long time, only his islands are full of monsters and the sea is full of perils, he doesn't get to choose the route, and the whole thing has been going on for about ten years when we meet him. Back in Ithaca, Penelope is waiting, batting off the attention of gold-digging suitors who want to marry a rich 'widow', by weaving (and secretly unweaving) material on her loom, telling them she'll only consider marriage when it's complete.

When I said that finding the beginning can be unclear, what I meant was maybe this was all just romanticised misattribution. An unreliable narrator, a false start. Maybe the real starting point had nothing much to do with that boy at all and was all about me. Maybe he was trying to be straightforward and I'd made it all mean something else. Perhaps the start was when I left my high-flying job just before the pandemic hit, with spooky timing. Now I was unemployed, worried about income and what to do with my time given I could not leave the house. The market had convulsed, no one was hiring. My one-bedroom flat, chosen to be as close to the city's heart as possible, felt stiflingly small and contained now London was on hold, now that there was nowhere to go except within its four walls. Without work, hard work, and lots of it, how should I spend these ever-elongating days? Purpose, as the ancients tell us in their annoyingly superior way, is important. Without it, I had nothing to gravitate my time around. I also felt a strange loss of self-esteem, work is an important part of my identity, I liked my job, I had been good at it, and now I felt its absence, I missed my team, connections, conversations, focus, building things.

Without work to distract me, my obsession deepened even as I knew it wasn't specifically about him, even as I understood it represented a generalised longing for connection. I composed and deleted messages, stayed up late and reread the script of our relationship, beginning to end, searching.

Every morning I woke face-creased, unrested. I had nothing to do. Home had turned into a prison and I had gone invisible. Everyone pulled into their nuclear families, bunkered down in survival mode. I called, but people were busy homeschooling their children, figuring out how to work remotely, no one had time to speak. The days felt endless, the month stretched out. Something caught deep in my throat, making it hard to swallow, harder to eat. For the first time I felt sharply lonely, unmoored. Or when it wasn't sharp, I felt like a green mosquito-infested pond somewhere deep in the woods, stagnating, dangerous. Whichever way you cut it, life was hardly going to plan personally or professionally. So maybe when I received that crappy break-up text it wasn't the start of anything much. Maybe everything was exaggerated, the timeline wasn't even that long, and I wasn't sliding into love, I just wanted to be, it was more that it would have been convenient. Maybe I wasn't all that surprised, and definitely not that heartbroken, just inconvenienced.

If you can't have romance then you can at least have comedy. So I went back to the dating apps, to have something to do as much as anything, and curated my life that way. I spent my days walking in circles, looping in endless one-hour increments through iterations of objectionable conversations with generic men, thankful for the mandatory two-metre distance rule. Mainly they talked and I listened. Mostly, it turned out, my views were not solicited at all.

'You're very intimidating.'

Was that a compliment? Should I try to be less than I am, to make your inadequacy more comfortable? The exchange felt exactly the opposite of the elegant Edwardian courtship promenades for which Victoria Park was designed, and it was the exact moment I gave up on trying to distance date in a pandemic. I committed to riding it out solo.

———————

I was washing food packaging and thinking, is this really scientifically proven? The shattering of the world, the shuttering of my city, the increasing social atomisation I had studied long ago in a very dull sociology course at university now hyper-accelerated. We were telling each other how boring the zombie apocalypse was. We'd prefer to be chased and gut-eaten. We'd prefer to outrun them, to have to cut off their heads with swords. We are social creatures, our little warm bodies are covered with soft, sensing skin. Being apart from each other was unnatural, painful. There's a reason people gather in cities, a reason solitary is the worst level of prison punishment. 'This is a breach of the Geneva Convention', screamed the outraged papers. The deep hole inside me had always been there but now it widened, glinted. My skin felt grey from touchless living, the opposite of all the tech-touch. My phone spooned into me, whispering, offering wisdom and despair.

One month became two. My friend Katharine was setting up a covid testing lab, was being useful, was saving lives, but in that gap of time, the vacuum of the world, I went into a strange, orbiting place.

I sat in the sunshine outside. I'd stopped washing my hair. I tried to rest in the bath but expensive oil elixirs didn't help. I lost the shape of myself, dissolving into the water. I bought a mini trampoline and bounced vertically, determined to manufacture endorphins if they wouldn't come naturally. I did yoga and lifted myself repeatedly into handstands in the upside-down world. I boiled eggs. Nothing helped. I was confronted with the age-old oppression of women, with total domestic terrorism. Cooking and cleaning, rinse and repeat. I stopped doing both. I stopped everything. It was startling the amount of dirt I generated, stuck here in my one-bedroom flat with nothing to do all day. I sat. In the sun. I waited. My eyes like piss-holes in the snow.

'Give me to drink Mandragora,' said Cleopatra, begging to be drugged, knocked out, sedated, 'that I might sleep out this great gap of time'.

'Sorry, love, we're all out of Mandragora, but the good news is we've restocked the loo roll.'

'Find the beginning.' Perhaps that wasn't the right beginning either. Let me find another. Maybe the true beginning did start with loss, but it wasn't a job loss, it was both a sharper and sea-deep kind, a slow sadness that sat underneath everything. In the beginning was my father and he was dying as slowly as he could, of cancer, not covid.

He was a doctor, a GP, so he understood everything. It was terminal, there was no hope of a cure, but his kind of cancer could be kept in check by various drug treatments. At this point it had been five years since he had first been diagnosed, and there was the promise of many more good years, if the treatments kept working. Anticipatory grief is what it's called when you know something bad will happen one day, an 'impending loss' is the name for when you know your father will die, not in the generalised sense that we're all going to die, but in a more concrete, specific way. Over time, I had learned to live with this slow unease behind everything: my father was in peril but there wasn't anything I could do, other than spend time with him, go on walks with him, make him laugh, and I now couldn't do any of this without risking his health: catching covid was a real concern as the treatments suppressed his immune system. Often it made me angry that he was told, was forced to live with this knowledge. I thought it would be better for him not to know, I wanted to protect him from having to keep having scans, keep being blasted with radioactive substances, having to weigh different treatment options. As the cancer slowly grew more aggressive he became more diplomatic, more equanimous. I was at his hospital bed after another difficult treatment, trying to make him laugh. I didn't realise yet this would be the last time I saw him for a long while.

The time before, I was walking with him the way we always walked together, only a little slower, and a much shorter route. It was early February and the woods weren't green yet. I pretended to take a photograph to allow him to pause and catch his breath. I left early to return to London to be cooked for and lied to. A choice I came to regret and later thought of often, twisting it this way and that like a stomach-knife. When the virus broke out my father became very fearful, stayed deep, burrowed in the quiet green countryside I grew up in, worried about dying extra-extra-early from covid, not cancer.

He understood the risk if he caught the virus: if intensive care places had to be triaged like rumours in the newspapers were suggesting, and doctors ended up having to choose who would get the next ventilator, he knew where he'd be on the list of priorities. So he banished everyone except my mother from his kingdom, and started to isolate before official regulations came in. He asked my brother and I to stay away from him for safety, we couldn't visit any more. I couldn't go back to my childhood home. I was an adult now anyway, had to face this by myself. As we spoke on the phone at night I tried to think of all the people who had it worse. I tried to imagine the people trapped on cruise ships in the middle of icy seas, especially the ones who'd saved all that money for a once in a lifetime trip to Antarctica, who were now confined to the windowless cabins they purchased with misplaced economy, with just an hour a day in the light, on the deck, because no countries would let the boats dock. I thought of teenagers caged inside without school, without friends, of bewildered people in care homes. I visualised it as clearly as I could but it didn't help all that much, thinking of those worse off. I knew I was lucky in so many ways but it wasn't much of a consolation – I was still enclosed within the confines of my own life, alone inside this horrible thing, I couldn't avoid the self-pity trap of my own petty issues: a break-up, no job, and a father I could no longer see – it seemed somehow to have a compounding effect inside the wider crisis of the world, even I saw the contradictions, the tension of it all. We are all so caught up inside ourselves.

That strangely sunny, optimistic spring full of flowers and birds slowly unfolded into a blazing summer. My neighbours had all been stress-gardening in our communal courtyard. Tending growing things seemed to comfort them and now there was colour everywhere I looked, blooms surrounded me, proudful strong white calla lilies, early pinking-red roses. The illegal dogs that should not live in our building were happier and more spoiled with every day that passed – they were having a reverse pandemic experience, no longer lonely and waiting all day for people to come home, now they belonged to all of us, were always in company. In contrast to the dogs, I felt more and more like I was suffocating, couldn't breathe, going transparent. Restrictions in London surged and eventually started easing a little as summer began to end.

It was near the end of a hot day when there was screaming on the street outside, screaming so loud I ran to investigate.

It was the familiar London conversational exchange, only the beeping and swearing were heightened, in both cadence and volume, because of the aggressive atmosphere, I guess. A man arched, like a puffing snake, hissing through the air at some other guy whose car was in his way. More cars got blocked in, more horns joined the chorus of discontent, and the emphasis subtly changed and charged. Fuck you. No fuck *you*. *Fuck* you. *Fuck you.* Eventually one of them gave way and precisely at the point where the two enemy cars passed each other, both with their windows open the better to hurl insults, with great precision, ballet-like timing and deadly aim, one man spat. A long jet of liquid arced through the open window and on to the other man's face. It was an impressive and devastating social commentary. A water pistol fired by a highly trained army sniper. Spitting at a total stranger for a minor inconvenience, in a pandemic of a respiratory airborne disease that we did not yet understand. Disgusting even in normal times, now weaponised, deliberate, intolerable. What if someone did that to my father? Suddenly, everything narrowed to a point. I couldn't breathe. Why did I live here? Society was broken. Everything was broken. I needed to get out of this horrible city. I turned away, turned to my computer, turned it into a magic carpet.

At this point, the UK had 'holiday corridors' open and people had gone away for summer holidays. I had some privilege, some savings, perhaps it was time to dip into them. I called my father to see what he thought.

'Go,' he said, 'after all, it's not like you're a doctor or anything useful.' This was the way we always talked, direct, sometimes combative, mostly designed to make each other laugh. My brother was a doctor, my mother was a nurse, I was the outlier.

'Will you promise not to get covid while I'm away? I don't want to worry about you.'

'I'll do my best. Just go – what else are you going to do? Mope around that tiny little flat by yourself?'

So perhaps that's how it began.

At this point Italy was on the list of safe countries and I consulted with my friend Lara about how best to avoid the romantic parts. I was keen to stay away from the tanned and beautiful honeymooning couples walking hand in hand on long beaches in white linen, blinding each other with sunlight catching on enormous, competitive diamonds, wanted whatever the opposite of the Amalfi coast was. She suggested I head out to a string of tiny volcanic islands off the coast of Sicily, and things clicked serendipitously. These islands, according to various theories, inspired part of *The Odyssey*, so I'd be tracing Odysseus's story in the real world, much to Emily Wilson's imagined disdain. I would follow him to his enchanted islands, see if I too could find the capricious gods, figure out if I could reconcile poetry to geography, maybe learn what monsters lurked in the seas between.

Grey-eyed Athena, goddess of wisdom and warfare, had a soft spot for Odysseus. She also had really good shoes. When the poem opens she's making the case to Zeus and the other gods that enough is enough and that Odysseus should be allowed to finally get home. As a first step, she makes the various gods agree to a plan to release him from Calypso's island where he's been held hostage for a pretty long time. Hermes, the messenger god, is dispatched to bring Calypso to heel and get her to set him free. Athena

> *tied her sandals on her feet,*
> *the marvellous golden sandals that she wears*
> *to travel sea and land, as fast as wind*

and she sprints off in a separate direction, over to Ithaca to catalyse Odysseus's awkward teenage son into taking action to find his father, the man who had left when he was a baby. He's a bit pathetic but Athena galvanises him. Once the 'owl-eyed' goddess has set things in motion, she flies away like a bird.

All I had to do by contrast to all this plotting was simply book a flight. I packed my suitcase full of whimsical white linen, enough for two weeks in the fierce Italian sun, and left the fear and static greyness of London behind me.

Then through the looking glass, down the rabbit hole, and I was sliding into the blue Tyrrhenian sea, feeling the weight, the salt and itch of it.

Chapter Two

The Floating Island of Aeolus

Aeolian Islands, Sicily, Italy

We reached the floating island of Aeolus,

… he agreed to help me, and he gave me

a bag of oxhide leather and he tied

the gusty winds inside it…

and he made Zephyr blow

so that the breath could carry home our ships

and us. But it was not to be

Odysseus

The Aeolian archipelago, just off the northern coast of Sicily, is made up of seven small volcanic islands. In Italian they are called the *Eolian* islands and when Italians say it, with a sort of sea sigh, 'eee-*Oh*-leon', it sounds like the wind blowing through the trees. Which is fitting, for this is the kingdom of Aeolus, the ruler of the winds.

Odysseus lands on Aeolus's 'floating island', feasts with him for a month, and is sent home on a fair wind with an actual gift bag. His nosy crew open it while he's sleeping, hoping for gold, but accidentally unleash the winds inside it, which blow their ship right back across the sea, just when they were in sight of home.

To reach these islets you no longer need to wait for the right kind of wind to fill your sails, just catch the next hydrofoil away from the ugly port city of Milazzo and head out towards the open sea.

Lipari, the largest island, is soft and romantic, all narrow roads, beautiful old street lights shining down on white marble stones, and the sound of bells shimmering through the air met by other bells. To me, it looked nothing like a prison, although the Italian Fascists felt otherwise – this was where they bunged their political opponents in exile in the 1920s.

When I arrived I felt like I was in some kind of inverted midsummer night dreaming world, that I'd slipped between realms, leaving fearful London for this bright and almost empty island. In real life, this place would be packed, but now the streets and beaches were almost deserted – no one had to compete for the choicest parasols closest to the water. The first thing I did once I'd dropped my bags was to go down to the sea, and when I sank into it for the first time, felt the weight of it, the waves touching my body, it seemed as though all at once I was coming back to myself, holding the shape of myself again. Something in me stretched out in the seawater and I promised myself that I'd swim every day, see every sunset, visit as many islands as I could, eat as much Italian food as possible. I was greedy for life again, wanted too much of everything.

I walked to the stationery shop where I became uncharacteristically slow. They didn't stock the pens I liked and in my haste I hadn't packed them, so I had to start from scratch and find a new kind. I've come to believe the bridge connecting my hand to paper is a serious thing. There's something kinaesthetic about handwriting, neurologically too – apparently it fires the brain in a different way to typing. I was trying out all the different pens for speed under the serious, owlish gaze of the wire-thin owner. He played his part perfectly, looking at me faintly anxiously after each test, in the way of a consulting doctor calibrating dosages. For me, it's all about the ink moving as fast as my thoughts across the page when I journal. I'm a bad student of Julia Cameron's morning pages – she suggests writing three full pages by hand first thing, and of Natalie Goldberg's timed writing exercises. I'd resisted them both for years but when my father was first told he had cancer, I picked up journaling properly, the same way I picked up crystals, deepened my yoga practice, and tried to meditate, suddenly more open-minded to anything other people had found helpful.

I selected some pens and the owner wrapped them carefully in an elegant twist of paper, and escorted me to the door with old-fashioned courtesy.

'If you like history,' he said slowly, in a way that made me think he was offering me something special, 'down this very old street is the house that Carlo Rosselli was held in. Not in prison but...' He paused to find the word. '... in exile, yes? He could not leave this place. You know Rosselli?'

I lied and nodded. I had no idea who Rosselli was but I didn't want to disappoint this kind and serious man who was telling me something important to him, something not every tourist who came here would know. I walked in the direction he pointed, and on the way looked up Rosselli.

Carlo Alberto Rosselli was an Italian anti-fascist and one of the founders of a clandestine publication. In 1926 he'd helped another leading socialist execute a daring escape to France, and was punished by being exiled here. He began writing *Liberal Socialism*, his most famous work, on Lipari and, eventually, he too made a daring escape, the way people did back then, to France and freedom. The house he'd been held in was on a dog-leg just off the main road near the cemetery, simple, white and plain. There was a plaque to his memory but it was small and easily missed. I wasn't sure what I'd been expecting, I guess being exiled to an island probably isn't as romantic as it sounds. I was glad he'd managed to escape.

Across the road was a *cimitero*, one of the prettiest words in Italian, I think, it sounds so cheerful, the way it's pronounced reminding me somehow of Mary Poppins. I walked over to look around, through the grand gates with their bowing angels. The graves were all lined up in rows facing the sea. Overhead power lines had been hacked and linked individually to each grave with what looked like incredibly unsafe electrical engineering. It meant each stone was illuminated with tiny lights, and most had a photograph embedded in the headstone, unlike English graves. Some of these photographs depicted the residents' oldest selves, the likenesses taken just before death, grim or stoic and resolute and old, others showed them in blazing youthful glory. I think I'd choose a blooming-youth picture, I'd be one of the pink cheeked, vain dead: remember me like this.

I wanted to swim before the day ended, I wanted to swim every chance I got. After being confined in my flat in London for so long I wanted to take up space in the world again. I caught the bus to Spiaggia di Canneto, the nearest beach, just as the sun started to unspool. The bus lumbered, annoying me, I was impatient to get to the sea, and then I got caught on a long call arranging some freelance work that delayed me getting into the water but which would mean I'd have an income for the first time in months. I felt the tension of it in my body, needing the work, wanting the sea. I hopped from leg to leg trying to get off the phone, watching the light bleed the sky blue. By the time I plunged in it was almost twilight and the seawater was early-autumn cool. My heart started to beat faster from the cold but by the time I'd counted slowly to one hundred and observed the burn slipping across my body, pinching and flaring over my collarbones, before moving into the deep creases of my elbows, I was calm and easy. This was the most peaceful meditative freedom I'd found, swimming alone as the sky darkened. Just the right hint of danger. I lay on my back and looked towards the pebbly beach, at the horizon, at the blue light falling into all the other blues. I like it best when everything smudges together, sea and sky, when you can watch the night falling into the water. There's something beautiful about night swimming, it feels transgressive, no one else on the beach or in the water, the sea darkening from translucent to opaque. It feels like adventure. I was floating against the tensile bounce of the waves, relaxed and easy, when I felt something whip across me.

Pain and panic. I gulped salt water and struck back for the shore, instinctively moving away from what I couldn't see, trying to understand how I could get an electric shock in water. It took my brain some seconds to catch up to the idea of a jellyfish, and I was suddenly sharply conscious that there was no one on the beach to call to for help if I needed it. Making it to the shallows, I ran across the stones and, shivering, examined the thick red marks spreading out across my shoulder. I'd never been stung before and it hurt more now that I was out of the water, a strange, hot, itching burn. Should I try to pee on myself? I consulted my phone which advised against it, instead instructing me to scrape the area with the edge of a credit card to remove the poison. Regardless, the marks continued to rise up, went ugly and dark-purple, the pain deepened into something that made me bite my lip. I realised later that I'd left my swimming costume behind somewhere on the pebbles in my rush to get back to town.

When I got back to my apartment, I video-called my nephew, Theo, who was four, and told him I'd been stung by a jellyfish. He was suitably impressed when I showed him my marks and we discussed which type of sting would hurt most, a jellyfish, a bee or falling into nettles. 'But then I would just get dock leaves,' he said, 'and it wouldn't hurt any more,' and he blew me a kiss through the phone and I said it felt much better, and wished it was all that simple.

At the restaurant that evening, a waiter noticed my still-burning raised marks with the actual kindness of strangers, the way Italians casually connect with you, the way Londoners never would.

'A *medusa* attacked you.'

I didn't know that the Italian for jellyfish was *medusa*.

Medusa's story isn't officially part of *The Odyssey* although there's a tenuous connection because Athena, goddess of war and wisdom, wears her severed head mounted on her shield. Medusa's story has more to it than the basics of coiling snake hair, turning men to stone, and being monstrous. She's deeply religious, a high priestess in training, a virgin. One day, I guess she's looking especially, provocatively devotional, perhaps that day her robes are also a bit shorter than usual. So, naturally, Poseidon rapes her. Right there on the temple steps. What choice did he have? It's not like she'd have said yes if he'd asked. She bleeds, it hurts. This is unforgivable – a terrible crime has been committed: Medusa has defiled Athena's temple. So in some classical victim-blaming moves, her rape is her fault, she is cursed with poison skin and given a head full of hair snakes, a fitting punishment for her trauma. Turned into a monster, exiled and later killed. It was ever thus with clever women. Her jellyfish namesakes, with their long stinging tentacles, keep the simplified version of Medusa's story alive – she's just a monster, forgetting the monstrous way she was turned into one.

The waiter took our order and left. I was having dinner with a guy I'd met on the ferry over here, in that incidental way that happens when you're both travelling alone. He was making me laugh with bad dating stories but I didn't want to share mine: the not-quite divorced man, the guy who got into poly because his girlfriend wanted to but she left him anyway, the boys with their externalised oozing wounds who said things like 'it's easier for girls' or 'I just want someone honest'. It would be so easy to twist them into comedy, play them for laughs, and usually I would but I didn't feel like turning my life into anecdotes and aphorisms to amuse a stranger. I wanted my boyfriend back, to be sitting across the table from him. He delighted in food, had a generous appetite for everything, he'd be figuring out how to recreate these recipes, making me order just one more dish to try, deliberating over which would be the most delicious wine.

The boat guy started casually touching me, a hand on my knee, my elbow, building towards something else, something I didn't want, touch at this time felt like an infraction and I left too abruptly, walking back to the apartment where I was staying with the moon shining on the white marble, with the church bells ringing out at odd hours. I was walking away from the port but if I listened I could still hear the insistency of the sea in the distance. Everything was quiet and full all at once. This time I was choosing solitude.

I sat in the moonlight on the outside steps that led up to the apartment, not wanting the night to end. Then I spoiled my own contentment by internet-stalking the boy I left behind, saw him in a hammock swinging over sapphiric water. The romantic in me wanted us to be swimming in the same sea – perhaps we were? I looked again but it was a Croatian island, so he was in the Adriatic and I was in the Tyrrhenian. My shoulder itched and burned and stung, the poisoned skin demanding attention, pulling me back to the present. I ran my hands over the raised parts, which were starting to blister, and forced my thoughts in another direction, calling to Aeolus, ruler of the winds, asking him to blow me a different way, spin me through space.

The days started to fuzz in that holiday-ish way. I wasted them perfectly in pursuit of small things. A particular picture-postcard view. Finding the ancient ruins and sitting watching a bird fly through the air with its shadow moving through the grass, wheeling

in circles around each other. Lighting a long yellow candle inside
the cathedral next to the church, bowing to my father's god, an
unbeliever with my inelegant, muttered prayer, my rosary string of
demands. I sat for a second in the empty wooden confessional booth
breathing in the incense, the smell of my childhood, the familiar
prickle of anxiety at the back of my neck at the idea of sins – it was
easier to atone for them back then. When I leave Lipari, I'll look
back at the castle on the hill and know that next to the castle is this
church, and in this church a candle burned.

Pasticceria Pesaresi made the best brioches in Sicily, or so they
claimed. Nothing like their dull French cousins, these were huge,
puff-light, and delicately flavoured with orange blossom. I cut
through the immense amounts of sugar with strong espressos that
soured my mouth, sharpened my mind and did something mildly
disconcerting to my heart rate. I was writing at the table outside at
the same time as trying to eat a *cassatella,* a puddingy biscuit famous
in Sicily: thin liquid ricotta enclosed in a sort of shortbread but it
puddled onto my plate, betraying me. How do Italian women eat
with such style?

Giuseppe La Greca (who turned out not to be Greek at all)
watched me from the next table with open amusement and
started talking in a way that always seems to happen when I write
in public places – as if it's an invitation, which it is, in a lot of
ways. He moved tables to join me, the easy way people do here,
the lightest of connection caught and returned. A bear of a man,

Giuseppe was a historian and a scholar. He'd written a book about all the people who'd been exiled here. There was a long list, 'An empress, mafia, criminals, liberals, anarchists, socialists, all kinds of people,' he said.

I said I had come here to the islands to find the sea-kingdom of the god Aeolus.

'But Aeolus was not a mythical character or a god! He was a real prince!' Giuseppe said, contending that he'd lived right here, on Lipari. Noticing my purple marks, he told me there was a relationship between Medusa and Aeolus which I didn't know about. 'You must check the wind and swim in the other direction. If the wind is blowing from the south, then you swim at the north coast, this way you avoid attacks.' He showed me which app to download. It had never occurred to me that winds and jellyfish were related. It had never occurred to me that I could check the direction of the wind, or that it would ever mean anything. I would come to learn much more about the importance of winds on islands, of the powers of Aeolus.

Lipari was for lovers – an island for swinging your hand into someone's, for kissing on street corners, for leaning across white tablecloths and putting food and fingers into his mouth, for drinking wine that stained your lips and swaying back down the streets, walking barefoot, heels hanging from fingertips, bodies touching. I liked travelling alone, how selfish I could be with the days: choice instead of compromise. I liked how much easier it was to meet people this way. At the same time, I wanted my ex-boyfriend to be here, and not ex- of anything. I was full of contradictions, tension, couldn't help it – it made me feel lonelier to be in this romantic place. I wanted him to eat brioches with me, to talk to strangers about gods and kings.

I sailed on to the next island, to Vulcano, with Aeolus's winds blowing around me, playing with my hair. The jellyfish sting had stopped hurting although the marks would not fade for weeks.

'What you're saying is inaccurate. This is not scientifically valid,' said the scientist, definitively.

'I'm just saying I *feel* more magnetic up here,' I said.

'But that's not how the magnetic field works.' He was looking at me with something like mild concern.

The volcanologist and I were standing at the summit of the volcano on imaginatively named Vulcano, the southernmost island in the chain. I had climbed the Fossa cone expecting glorious solitude and unbroken silence, and of course there was an actual volcanologist at the top, and of course he was messing around with a buzzy drone.

Around us sulphuric gases belched out stink yellow, drifting upwards towards the bright sky. The whole island reeked of this heavy incense, it smelt faintly medicinal and made me feel as if I was inside some kind of mediaeval apothecary in search of an unpleasant cure. The ancient Greeks believed that sulphur had cleansing properties and absorbed negative energies. After Odysseus makes it home at the end of the story he goes on a killing spree of his wife's prospective boyfriends, the suitors, who've been trying to seduce the rich 'widow'. When he's finished, they're all dead, the hall is covered in blood and Odysseus asks a servant to

bring me fire
and sulphur as, a cure for evil things,
and I will fumigate the house

Under our feet the volcano was grey and grainy and crumbly. It seemed to me to be composed mostly from gravel and looked pleasingly like a textbook illustration of a classical volcano, with all the things you'd expect, a sunken 'caldera', the bit where the top has blown off, and yellow puffs of smoke. I scratched at the bites on my legs compulsively. The mosquitoes on this island were small and violently aggressive, perhaps it was all that sulphur in the air. My volcanologist was now gazing up at the sky, flying his drone to gather data points that might help explain when the volcano was next going to explode. He told me the scientific community were concerned because an explosion here was extremely overdue. According to their predictions, this volcano should explode once every hundred years, but the last one was back in 1890, and no one was sure what was going on. All over the straggly little town below us at the foot of the mountain there were brightly coloured graphic posters which merrily depicted how, in the event of an explosion, the local population would absolutely be able to safely evacuate very calmly and straightforwardly, and definitely wouldn't be boiled alive by hot lava flowing at high speed down the mountain. They shared the same illustrated enthusiasm and wild optimism of those comic strips tucked into the front pouches of aeroplane seats, showing how inflatable slides will puff yellow and magically transform into lifeboats to save us all when the plane falls out of the sky, which they prefer to call 'in the event of a water landing'.

I pulled a necklace and some earrings out of my rucksack and put them down on the crater ridge.

He looked at me.

'What are you doing?'

'Charging my crystals.'

He rolled his eyes. 'I suggest you pick those up – sulphur will tarnish silver. Now, *that* is a scientific fact.' He started laughing.

'It's a weird time, we need science, crystals, all of it,' I said, putting them back in my bag as he grinned at me. I asked him to stop flying the noisy drone for a bit so we could enjoy the silence up here. In the quiet we looked out to sea back at Lipari, across the water, interrupting the horizon.

Apart from taunting scientists there wasn't much else to do on this island. The landscape as I looked out was barren and stark, had something lunar about it. Vulcano is famous for its healing mud baths but they were closed for renovation so instead I rented a bicycle from a shop that mostly rented out scooters, which should have been a warning sign, and cycled over to Valle dei Mostri ('Valley of the Monsters') on the north-east coast. It was a much harder ride than it looked on the map, mostly uphill through the oddly empty landscape with the heavy sun beating down. Most of the ascents were so steep I had to get off to walk, sweating in failure alongside the bike. When I arrived, it wasn't a valley, nor were there any monsters, just a grassy area at the top of some sea cliffs where rocks formed from boiling lava had been frozen into huge weird shapes as they cooled.

I hoisted myself up onto the darkness of one of the largest stones and attempted to meditate, but ended up just staring out at the blue sea. I thought of my father sitting in the kitchen that looked out on to the garden, tended to with obsessive care by my mother during lockdown. There would be flowers everywhere, and on his worst days, on the days between treatments when he couldn't get up the energy for a real walk, I knew she'd always encourage him to take a turn around the garden, 'get some fresh air, you'll feel better' was her mantra. I knew the effort too. I could see her pointing out particular flowers to him, the beginnings of vegetables, talking away to compensate, filling the spaces, both of them pretending that he wasn't in pain.

When I left, I stacked some smaller rocks together, an offering of thanks to something I didn't understand, for being able to travel again, for escaping the sadness bound up in London.

At Ristorante La Forgia Maurizio, Maurizio himself – owner, chef, raconteur – conducted a detailed consultation at my table which seemed to involve a sort of psychological profiling, and declared he would choose my food for me, like some dominant lover on an early date, based on my chakras or whatever psychic propensities that he'd discerned. Small things arrived first, two sour olives, a piece of ricotta cheese rolled in herbs, a miniscule slice of wild fennel tortilla, an egg cup full of a dark soup made from black lentil and barley spelt to which I was given a doll's spoon and instructed to add olive oil and nigella seeds. A seafood pasta pink with tomatoes, supposedly a half-portion but enormous, unctuous, delicious, and last, a shot glass of sweet Malvasia wine accompanied by a box of miniature biscotti for dipping. The warmth of the wine and sugar pooled through my blood. Whatever magical powers he'd used to divine what I liked to eat, Maurizio had got everything exactly right. The meal was better than anything I had imagined Sicilian food to be. DREAM instructed the Illy espresso cup, white on yellow. I squinted at it for a while before getting it. Instructions from motivational crockery were not what I needed right now (or ever).

'Your feelings? You're writing about your feelings?' I was writing in my journal after dinner and a beautiful Italian man was flirting or trying to, and I, usually confident, usually able to speak to anyone, was fluttersome, fumbling. Out of practice. Blushing and unlike myself. He smiled at me uncertainly. A connection almost made.

I walked down to the dark beach, the moon glowing, thinking of my hand being held at the cinema, across restaurant tables, on the sofa. The meal had been better than I could have imagined, my ex-boyfriend had turned out to be very different from what I'd imagined. There was a heaviness in that. Sadness and self-flagellation, how had I not seen it? And why was I still thinking about someone who had proven themselves inadequate, unsatisfactory, unknowable? I knew I was wasting my own time, the same way he'd wasted it, and still I wanted him, was still checking for a text. It made me hot and angry and small and sad. It made me everything all together. I took off my shoes and walked ankle-deep in the sea all the way along the shore.

My phone pinged. But of course it wasn't him – the phone was nothing if not a master of psychological torment. A photograph popped up, *On this day two years ago:* my father walking in Oxfordshire, looking well, looking mildly ironic. It stopped me in my tracks like a cartoon cat, paw paused, absurdly airborne. He looked exactly like himself, very different to how he looked now. I hadn't noticed the incremental changes, I hadn't paid enough attention.

In the picture we are walking across those classical-green English fields, over to the ruins of a Roman villa. It is trying to intimidate us with the permanence of its impermanence, still here, even if ruined. We ignore it, we're too busy talking.

'Could you imagine your mother with anyone else?'

'No, but you need to write that down and give her permission,' I say, 'these kinds of things need to be written down.'

There's a pause. A long one, the way it's always been with him.

'I've been thinking of asking you to write my wedding speech,' I tell the back of him, recognising the irony as soon as I say it. It's stupid because I'm not, and have never been, a wedding, ring, property-promises kind of girl. Conventional things I'm supposed to want turn my stomach, feel pressured and odd and false. Perhaps it's just the fantasy of that role space – the seminal father-daughter moment. I know it's a flawed premise, there are not exactly suitors lining up for my hand. Still, I want this for a future that might come, a future that he might not be in. My love is expressed in language, has always been verbal, I like the way words weave shawls around us. And he too loves speechifying, takes it seriously, edits for weeks. This time it's not a pause. It's a silence, denser, softer. My father stops walking and I stop too. He turns to me.

'Yeah,' he says, 'I can do that,' and he turns his fist into a microphone, and clears his throat.

Above him, birds swoop the sky, the sun is shining as I wait for him to speak.

'Laura is/was my daughter,' says my father, 'her behaviour has been satisfactory...' He pauses and smiles. '... for the most part.' And we laugh and the grass is summer green and the air is soft. It's a shard but I'll take it.

My request that I'd screwed up courage to ask, turned into a joke. Is/was. The slash, delicate and slight against the liminal space on each side. The present/past.

The phone pinged again, bringing me back: a company had offered me a short-term contract. It felt like a gift. It would be fully remote and I could start when I got home. My shoulders dropped.

I'd heard that Salina was the opposite of Vulcano, lush and luxurious, and I caught the next boat over there, still scratching at my mosquito bites, temporary blemishes, a raised reminder of where I'd been. The greenest island in the archipelago, it was named after the salt lake that still scented the air as I walked through the town of Santa Marina to find a taxi.

This island is obsessively proud of three things: capers, Malvasia wine and its cinematic associations. The Oscar winning film *Il Postino* was shot here – something the islanders still boast about, leaving out the part that the famous beach featured in the movie was washed away by the sea years ago.

I'd splurged and booked an elegant hotel: white linen, long terraces with muted fabric hammocks and those four-poster beds with floaty curtains set around an infinity pool. I had thought it was supposed to be adult-only but as I checked in a pair of kids were screaming and running around. It's horrible enough being on holiday with other people's children, insufferable when they're over privileged and spoilt, intolerable when they're a breach of policy. The manager shrugged. They hadn't told her they were bringing children. What could she do? A reminder to read the small print: it was 'adult only' *and* they accepted one child per booking over the age of twelve. I was confused. I swung in a hammock attempting to ignore the yelling and splashing, trying to practise acceptance. I failed to accept. I texted Rachel complaining about the children. She texted back a picture of her bump. Her pregnancy was a total abstraction for me, rather than something embodied – due to lockdown and her own caution I hadn't seen her for months.

I've been reading parenting books, she wrote. *This insistence on natural birth is toxic. Shaming women if they can't. Trapping ourselves within patriarchal ideas of suffering and domestic place. Amazing that women's liberation has brought us to the extreme that motherhood is the coolest thing to do in your life.* She added the rolled-eyes emoji but I knew she was really excited to be pregnant, it had been years of trying.

Just don't bring your baby to adult-only hotels, I texted as the screaming reached fever pitch.

Promise, she wrote.

Spiaggia dello Scario was a short walk from the hotel through the village of Malfa with its yellow and pink houses, scooters and cafes, churches and vineyards. A simple cove with large white stones, it curved around a denim sea that was flat, almost unmoving. I walked across the rocks and slipped into the dark blue water just as a woman ran out shrieking – a jellyfish early-warning system. Fearing *medusa*, remembering Giuseppe's advice, I sprang out of the water and headed over to the other coast.

Rinella is a fishing village where the boats bob, the sand is black and the living is easy. Something like that. Only it was deserted and the beach looked a bit dystopian. Pa.Pe.Ro., the renowned restaurant, was closed for a private event, but I begged and eventually they allowed me to buy a glass of their famous ricotta and sweet-caper granita. Sounded revolting, tasted extraordinary. Before I came here I didn't know what granita was. In between ice cream and sorbet, it was better than both – the ricotta gave a grainy sweetness to the ice, and the capers were marinated in honey and thyme to make them sticky and chewy.

A day at the seaside with an ice cream – what could be nicer? It wasn't so much *la dolce vita* but *dolce far niente* (the sweetness of doing nothing) that I was falling for in these islands. After the last lick I walked across the black sand and straight into the sea, defying that old childhood rule of waiting to digest. I wanted to be buoyant, to slide out of my body and feel my ribs stretch and curl as I swam out towards the horizon. I rolled over and over in the waves until I was dizzy, spinning sky into water and cliff into liquid.

That evening there was a kind of sea-fog oppression in the weather system and a strange, hot wind came that ruffled the air around me but didn't cool as it blew. There are eight kinds of winds that Aeolus presides over. This one was *scirocco,* a southerly wind that blows in from the Sahara making everything feel sultry and close. It quickly became sweltering and humid and guests lay unmoving around the pool. I slept too heavily and fractiously all at once. Winds on islands affect you strongly, I was learning. *Scirocco* is associated with causing feelings of unease and irritation in people, it also supposedly causes insomnia. In me, it succeeded in achieving all of these things.

Salina did not charm me despite its verdant prettiness and its sweet pebbly cove. It was too groomed, too self-aware, too luxurious. I was impatient to keep moving, I was speeding up again after all the stillness and screaming slowness, winding my energy back up, starting to feel normal, back to my regular fast way of moving through the world.

There was enough time to visit one final island. I boarded the hydrofoil again and headed out towards one of the wildest and furthest-flung islands in the archipelago.

From the sea, Stromboli looks like a child's drawing of an island, a triangular green mountain rising straight up from the water. Less than twelve square kilometres with about five hundred residents, it is mostly vertical. The skyline is dominated from every angle by the volcano which extends nearly a thousand feet above sea level, and is one of the most active in the world. Stromboli – confusingly, the name of the volcano as well as the actual island, there not being much to distinguish the one from the other, I guess – has been pretty much constantly erupting for the last five thousand years and sees no reason to stop now.

The ancient Greek geographer Strabo wrote, 'it is here they say that Æolus resided', and perhaps he was right, there was a particular energy on Stromboli that made me feel free and easy. It felt like a place a god could live. The island was so small that I could hear the sea from anywhere, the same way that everywhere I looked was the volcano. It was wild and wildly elemental.

Sea noise rocked me to sleep in the guesthouse where I was staying, and in the morning I woke to a picture perfect view of the volcano from the garden, framed by bursting orange trees like a Cezanne painting. I ate breakfast at a blue-painted table set out under the vines, fresh orange juice made from fruit taken from the trees, with home-made bread and jam and strong coffee, gave thanks for being in the land of culinary delights, and walked down to Spiaggia Lunga for a swim. The beach wasn't enticing, it was a sort of gritty grey sand. Stromboli evidently was not an island for water and swimming, it was a place to climb up high, an island of air, fire and earth.

I started walking up the volcano as the day cooled into the afternoon, hiking slowly through olive trees and oleanders on the lower slopes, watching as the sunset extruded across the horizon, rich orange shifting to faintest pink. It was a long walk, about six hours in total, but I took it slowly and looked at everything. The scent of *Cestrum nocturnum* perfumed the air – part of the jasmine family, it seemed to me like the devoted youngest child of the volcano with its green-white flowers that bloom only after the sun sets, scenting the air extravagantly. The sea at the foot of the mountain crashed again and again against the solidity of the volcano that pushed its way up from under the water. There was quiet reverence inside me as I walked. A spinning inwards and a stilling, even as my eyes caught on all the trees and flowers and the dance of the sea and the light falling, as I climbed higher and afternoon turned to night.

At the top I lay on my back gazing up at the sky. The dome of constellations reached down towards the sea and shooting stars fell across the darkness. The only sound was the waves lapping against the foot of the volcano far beneath me. If I turned my head to the left, I could see the fire darts that restless Stromboli was shooting upwards in spurts, and tiny lights dotted all along the mountainside – the torches of other hikers, watching the explosions alongside me in spiritual pilgrimage. It was so beautiful. Tears poured down my face but luckily it was too dark for anyone to see. I wasn't sure why I was crying – for the world in all its sadness at this time of grief, for the wild beauty right here alongside it, for my father, for myself, for love, for all of it. 'Those old saints bless us every chance they get,' says the dying priest to his young son in *Gilead*, the last book I'd read. The phrase stuck with me. This was a blessing, a benediction. There were so many stars and it's easy to forget they're always with us, burning all the time, until we see them shining through clear and perfect darkness and catch our breath and remember.

I once had a boyfriend who believed strongly that a person should never repeat anything. His philosophy was that astonishing food in amazing restaurants and other transportive experiences should be enjoyed as a one-off, they can never possibly be as good the second time, you can't ever recapture that first feeling, delight is echoed at best and disappoints at worst. I thought of him the next day, as

I prepared to hike up again, the same volcano, the second day in a row. I thought of him and I missed how sweet he had been to me, the whole time we were together. His was a generous sort of kindness and it stretched out into the aftermath of our break-up too. He had been right about many things but his philosophy didn't hold this time. The walk was just as beautiful, the sky garlanded with a new mixture of pinks and blues, the wind moving softly through the trees again, the mountain just as stern and unforgiving. I lay down in the dirt near the viewing platform and rubbed soil into my hands, I wanted to get animal-low and close to it. I sent different prayers to different gods, mostly forms of 'thank you' for being here, for this beauty, for the wonderment. I looked up into the dark stars and thought how quickly things can change and how long everything can stay the same. The stars didn't twinkle but rather glowed in constellations tessellating across the darkness. Star maps in the sky spelling fortunes. Not that I could read what they were saying or decipher their patterns. I like the idea of astrology, the moving wheels of it, the houses, stars gliding across the darkness, whispering our fates as planets conjoin, the thought that things can be foretold, predicted and known, that life can spin on a sixpence, if you pull the right cards. A fortune teller once told me that I was born under a balsamic moon, straddling the need to resolve the past while preparing for the future. Something in that rang true but these things are designed to be broadly appealing. I looked up at the maps lacing the sky, at the arrangement of the stars, wanting reassurance that things would get better, that life would open again.

The next day I went searching for a hidden graveyard which Pasquale, from the guest house, had casually told me about with astonishingly vague directions. I liked how these missions turned baggy holiday days purposeful, of hunting out the hidden, seeing what other people missed. I already knew the main cemetery was on the mountainside above the town, neat and orderly, because I'd seen it from my hikes, but superstitions meant that plague victims could not be buried with the others, so their graveyard was separate. It had felt fitting at this time of new plague to pay homage to the past ones, but I'd searched for hours and now it was hot and I was sweating. I looped again back around the path that came off the mountain to see if I could find a track but there was nothing but high yellow grass and panting heat coming off the trail. No clear way forward. I decided to try a different route, from Piscità beach.

At the top of a rocky scrabble strewn with broken beer-bottle glass and half hidden by bushes, I found six small graves looking out to sea. The afternoon sun gilded the white cross on the largest grave and fired the long grass behind the stones, turning it golden. Some graves had stacks of rocks on them, green sea glass, broken tiles. They were taken care of. There must have been an access track I missed. I sat for a long time in the peace here, looking out to sea. In front of me was sweetly named Strombolicchio, a small, uninhabited rocky island just out from the bay, once the proud top of the volcano, until it was blown off in an explosion. The sun was dipping and there was one more place I needed to find.

I wasn't quite sure if I was in the right spot. A practical rather than an existential question this time. According to the map I was standing by Aeolus's cave. It seemed unlikely that the ruler of the winds would have chosen this unprepossessing place, a basic dark opening on a sea cliff, but the map was insistent.

In the story Aeolus has a 'fine citadel', a 'palace' behind a wall of solid bronze, very different from this cave. I sat for a while on the rocks as my mind circled in its annoying, obsessive way, back to the beginning, back to the boy I had been dating. I reread the fish-gut text he sent me and my response. I was happy with the way I said things, a small thing, but I'd take it. I still wanted him to call me, text me, surprise me by arriving here in a huge romantic gesture, which was completely absurd as he didn't know where I was. The wind blew through the cave, telling me to let go. Easy for Aeolus to instruct. He was a god, I'm a mere mortal.

It was early evening at the waterfront cafe, mosquito hour, my last night on Stromboli. My flight home was in a few days and I needed to set sail tomorrow. I sipped my wine and read *The Group*, a book about a set of university friends. It was deftly written and made me long to go back to forever, which was what it all felt like then, in my bursting early twenties. This sentence made me ache: 'he said I liked watching my girlfriend swimming. I liked him using the word, and liked him watching, and with the sun shining it felt like perhaps I could be claimed'. Was I waiting to be claimed? It felt too passive but there was part of me that still wanted to be rescued, that was still waiting for a text. But there was no point in waiting for anything any more. Take action. Move. Move on.

In my journal I made a list of all the beaches I'd swum at on this trip, ranking them according to inconsistent criteria, listed my flaws (many) and possible mitigation strategies (meditation?). The wind ruffled my pages and I watched how the waves embodied it, gave shape to air, and felt a sharp anticipatory longing for 'the endless immensity of the sea' even though it was here, crashing up against the rocks, right alongside me.

These volcanic, windswept islands had reset me, a tonic for troubled times: volatile, unstable, mysterious. Between the wind and water, fire and earth, I felt elemental, wild, less on edge even while the world remained uncertain, explosive, a snow globe of panic and fear. I'd shaken off the grey torpor, the nigglethinking of London.

My body had strengthened from all the hiking and swimming. I had started to gather my powers back to myself.

On Stromboli I found what I was looking for and I didn't want to leave, but time was flowing, my flight home was soon, so I sailed back, over to the mainland.

Chapter Three

The Island of the Sun God

Sicily, Italy

the Sun leapt up
into the sky of bronze, to shine his light
for gods and mortals on the fertile earth

I took the hydrofoil from the islands back to Sicily, caught a train that rumbled slowly along the coast towards Cefalù, an old fishing town, and walked from the station through the narrowing mediaeval streets in search of Agrodolce, which translated as bittersweet, aptly named for these strange times.

Some scholars believe that Sicily was the inspiration for the island of the sun god in *The Odyssey*. The quality of the sunlight here is supposedly scientifically distinctive – something about the combination of low levels of water vapour, the location of the island and its atmospheric clarity means the light is less diffuse here – in other words, it blazes. Sicily is sticky with sun, streaming more than two thousand hours of it a year, so it makes sense to me that this could be Helius's island.

Helius, the sun god, had a thing about cows. He kept herds of white oxen on his island and prized them above all else. The enchantress Circe and the prophet Tiresias both warn Odysseus not to set foot on this island, but his exhausted crew persuade him to drop anchor for the night. Zeus sends an 'eerie storm', the ship is grounded for weeks, and food starts running out. Odysseus strides away to pray for guidance, foolishly leaving his starving men (*Harvard Business Review* would take issue with much of his leadership style). The men reckon it'd probably be okay to eat a cow or two on balance, reasoning that they can always make amends by building a temple to Helius later, and anyway it'd be better to be killed than die of hunger. They make fast work of butchering the animals, and are feasting on delicious barbequed beef by the time Odysseus returns.

Helius, hugely offended, fragile masculinity being what it is even for gods, sulks. He threatens to stop shining on earth unless something is done, and weird as his cow thing is, the rest of the gods don't feel like living in darkness. So, when Odysseus sets sail again,

Zeus hurls a few signature thunderbolts, destroying the ship, and the crew either fall overboard and drown in a whirlpool, get their skulls crushed in by falling masts, or are eaten by a sea monster. In a twist no one saw coming, only Odysseus is left pacing around the deck in a tizz, trying to figure out how to survive a whirlpool on one side and a ravenous sea monster on the other. The answer, as it so often is in life, is to cling to a fig tree.

Agrodolce was a boutique hotel on the highest floor of an ancient building with no lift. I sweated my way up the steps, dragging my red suitcase, while from the top of the stairs, Rita laughed down at me. She was short and curvy with dark hair and a flashing warmth.

Trained as an architect, she'd renovated this space herself, right down to painting the blue and yellow tiles that decorated the central kitchen in the communal area. Rita did everything, even baking the fresh *mamalata* tarts each day for breakfast, criss-crossed with intricate lattice patterns, a different jam and a different pattern every day. I ate them on the narrow *terrazza* surrounded by perilously balanced succulents. Rita kept encouraging me to eat too many tarts, drink too much espresso.

Lovely as the hotel was, I didn't want to be back on the mainland – even though Sicily is technically an island, even though the long curve of the sandy beach was just steps away – because it meant everything would be ending soon. I've never been much good at endings, and it was worse this time. I felt stricken, suffocated at the idea of going home in a couple of days, more than just the normal dread of a holiday ending, a sense of an escape drawing to a close, of handing myself in. London was becoming dangerously infected and I was afraid of being caught in another lockdown alone, of trading freedom for imprisonment, worried I would be going back to a certain kind of sadness, that I would likely become sick. I'd lost the gods too, I no longer felt windborne and airy but grounded again, pinned by gravity. I pushed these thoughts away as I walked through the streets.

Cefalù is an ancient town stuffed full of Arab-Norman architecture, and like most Italian cities, had too many beautiful old buildings, divine churches, extraordinary architectural wonders to take in.

The cathedral in the main square was built as part of a bargain with Jesus Christ. Ruggero II, king of Sicily, was caught in a huge storm at sea, begged god to save him and in return promised to build a church to his glory. Next thing he knew, he was washed up on the soft sand of Cefalù's beach, instead of drowned at the bottom of the ocean. He kept his end of the deal, started construction, and persuaded artisans from Constantinople to come over and install a complicated Byzantine-style golden mosaic in the domed ceiling. I looked up at it, a portrait of Cristo Pantocratore (Christ all powerful), and one of the finest examples in all of Sicily, apparently. Christ was having a good hair day, sporting a hipster beard, and seemed to be wearing his mother's blue robes. Almost nine hundred years later and the golden tiles still shone brightly. Christ looked down at me, stern and radiant as ever. I bought a postcard to send to my father but forgot to send it.

Later I'll find it wedged between pages in a book. Christ will look impassively at me again, holding his fingers in a complicated arrangement that is somehow more noticeable on the card than it was in the ceiling. Thumb touching the little and ring finger, making a circle, middle finger slightly bent, submissive to the outstretched index finger pointing up. Representing the letters IC, X and C to create the Christogram ICXC, meaning 'Jesus Christ'. Just in case there could be any possible confusion.

My family are Irish Catholic and I went to church until the age of seven, at which point my faith stretched and broke after I was instructed in 'transubstantiation', the mystery rather than the symbology of the bread and wine. I couldn't quite believe in bodies and blood so I stopped going to mass entirely and stayed at home, preferring the exoticism of being alone in a quiet house. Before I stopped going, the part of the Catholic Mass I liked best was the bit when people stand up, shake hands with strangers across and behind the pews, wishing each other peace. It's a scripted conversation. 'And also with you' is the refrain. I will think about all this as I arrange my fingers to mirror Christ's sign language and hold them back up to him. 'Peace be with you,' I'll whisper. Jesus will remain silent.

The divine sits alongside the ordinary. From the cathedral I walked towards the Lavatoio Medievale (a mediaeval laundromat). A stone staircase led down from the street to a covered area where a series of shallow stone troughs were carved, each with a ridged washboard set like a pillow at one end, to scrub the clothes as they soaked. I could feel the oppression of women throughout the ages as I walked around them getting my shoes wet. Legend says that the river Cefalino, which flows through here to fill the troughs before continuing out to sea, was formed from the tears of a nymph who accidentally killed her lover.

At the top of the steps a stone had been engraved – the text was in Latin but there was a translation: *Here flows Cefalino... purer than silver, colder than snow.* Purer than silver, colder than snow. I loved the romance, the cadence of it, even if it was a fairy tale of domesticity.

I was putting my own laundry out to dry in the sun up on Rita's rooftop terrace, *just like a real Italian girl,* I was thinking, when I fumbled, dropped a sock and watched it land on the red terracotta tiles of the roof below, *very unlike a real Italian girl.* There was no way to get down there so I mentally consigned it to the kingdom of odd socks, but Rita was not about to let that happen.

'We will use something made by Santina, my grandmother,' she said cryptically, pulling out what appeared to be a large piece of cardboard from a cupboard behind reception. '*Allora,* we will go fishing. *Attenzione!* Be careful!'

She put a miniature mace into my palm. Santina had seemingly joined together four separate types of vicious fish hooks, glued them to a heavy lead fishing weight, attached it to fishing line, and wrapped that around the cardboard to keep it from tangling. She was clearly not the sort of woman who would let laundry or anything else get away from her. I lowered the mace on its fishing line down onto the roof while Rita filmed me on her phone.

'Lao-ra, what are you doing?'

In the video you can see my bare feet on the marble terrace, terracotta roofs bright against the blue sky. White legs, my pink skirt moving in the breeze. The camera pans up to my face.

I'm wearing a mask but you can tell I'm smiling.

'We're going sock fishing.'

By the grace of some minor Italian god, or more likely guided by the ghost of ancient Santina, I miraculously managed to snag the errant sock on my first go, and hauled it up to rapturous enthusiasm from Rita, who'd been commentating all the time like a football pundit, with the fast-paced ebullience I so loved in the Italians. It sounded to me like they always spoke in italics.

'*Brava, Lao-ra! Brava! La prima tentativo! Va bene!*' You can hear Rita laughing behind the camera.

I sent the video to my father thinking he'd find it funny, but he didn't reply, which was unusual. Instead my mother messaged to say that the new drugs were making him feel sick. My parents had met at the doctors and nurses ball when they were both students and been married more than forty years. She was his protector and occasional spokesperson these days, and I knew living under his totalitarian covid regime was taking its toll. He was very afraid of catching the virus and had put in place stricter rules than the government. Not being able to see my brother or hug my little nephew, Theo, was hard for her. She loved to cook and I wanted to cheer her up so I persuaded Rita to write down the recipe for the delicious jam tarts and texted it to her along with a photograph, for inspiration.

In a world without hotels, Emily Wilson explains Odysseus had to rely on a code of 'guest-friendship' called *xenia*. In the poem, guests are usually treated extremely well, given a hot bath, massaged with oil, provided with a feast and the softest bed, before being plied with lavish gifts and sent on their way. In return they provide amusement and news in the form of stories over dinner. However, there are also a series of violations of the code, with abusive guests and bad hosts who imprison the crew, put spells on them, and in some cases eat them.

I violated my part of the guest code by asking for a swimming towel, causing Rita to turn into every stereotype of an overbearing Italian mother. She refused to give me one. Why would I want one? It was *Ottobre*, far too cold. She forbade it. I must not swim. I'd catch a cold or covid, or worse. I eventually persuaded her to hand over an orange towel and she flung it at me theatrically, remained highly disapproving, tutting every time I returned with the back of my hair salt wet from the rough, demanding sea, and then undermined the whole performance by smiling at me.

Physiologically I'm lucky, I've always been pretty balanced, I exercise often and my body works in a faithful, animalistic way. I've grown to understand how it talks to me, its alerting system, but I had not realised it needed so much light. My nails and hair quickened and it felt like my mind was clearing and strengthening after the anxious, spinning thoughts of lockdown. Energy buzzed through me again, and it was more than the strong Italian coffee, it was this fierce, blazing, beautiful sunlight.

I caught a bus up the mountain to Castelbuono. A small village with a pink castle that reminded me of the jewellery boxes of my girlhood, the ones that played music and had a ballerina who twirled if you twisted a key, the type I'd craved so badly as a child. Inside the castle was what I'd come to see, the Cappella Palatina. The chapel was Sicilian baroque at its most bonkers. A mad whirling mix of white stucco carvings of angels and animals, mythological creatures and grotesque lunatic figures against a solid gold background. It looked like crazy three-dimensional wallpaper, the sort you'd find in a money-laundering billionaire's mansion. The creatures cavorted around the walls chuckling and grimacing while the skull of Saint Anne watched empty-eyed from her silver cage behind the altar. Maximum strength religiosity. There was something uplifting about how silly it was.

The guidebook had mentioned some paintings hidden in a crypt in the church on the main square. I followed the small stone steps down beneath the altar but couldn't find the light switch so used my phone torch to look at the secret frescos. They dated from the Middle Ages and the biggest one was a painting of a village scene with skeletal people all getting out of their coffins. I guessed it was Judgement Day and supposed to be comforting and hopeful but it was creepy, especially by torchlight. According to legend this was a place of miracles, so averting my eyes from the skeletons clambering around, I whispered a prayer for my father, who believed in Catholicism, in its perfumed mysticism, its sacred symbols. I always said the same thing, the same incantation to his god, asking for more time, for the treatment to work as well as it could. I never asked for a cure. Even gods have limits. It was damp down here and cold. I was glad to come back out into the sunshine. I sat on the church steps watching donkeys turned into binmen moving up and down the narrow streets that were too small for cars, collecting rubbish. The donkeys looked pissed off.

I had openly admitted my hatred of all things fungi, and the waiter immediately reported me to Giuseppe, the owner of Nangalarruni, who came out to my table on the street already throwing up his hands in horror before we'd even exchanged a word. When I had eaten his pasta, he shouted, I would be humbled, on my knees, forced to admit the errors of my ways, I would beg for forgiveness, for absolution for my sins. I smiled at him, pretty sure it'd be the other way around. We had a deal.

'So, *va bene*, I will choose what you eat. A pasta.'

'*Sì*. But does this pasta have mushrooms?'

'Yes.'

'But I don't like mushrooms.'

'Impossible. Then you will see!'

'Do you use a pig to find them?'

'A pig?' He looked disgusted, I'd managed to insult him again. 'Only the French use pigs. I use only a dog, of course!'

He returned with a plate of *spaghetti cacio, pepe e funghi di bosco* made with *la mazza di tamburo*, which my phone translated as 'one of the most showy, known and appreciated edible mushrooms'. I wasn't allowed to choose my drink either, a glass of wine arrived, slammed down by Giuseppe who watched with a scowl as I spun my fork and took a mouthful.

'*Allora.* So?'

A lifetime of bias erased in a bite of pasta. The mushrooms were unlike any I'd tried before, delicate and tasting of deep dark woods. The spaghetti silken not creamy. I was wrong. And sorry. Giuseppe nodded in benediction.

Placated, he brought out a huge silver platter piled with all the different kinds of mushrooms from the kitchen and sat next to me, holding each one affectionately, telling me their names, where to find them in the woods, and their unit costs. He unwrapped valuable rare truffles from their muslin coverings with great care, as if they were sleeping babies. I wrinkled my nose at the strong smell.

'Will you take a photograph of me and the mushrooms, Giuseppe?'

'*Va bene.*'

There I am, wearing my father's panama hat set at a jaunty angle, a turquoise jumper, long dark hair flowing down my left shoulder, an enormous, ridiculous plate of raw mushrooms before me, raising my fork and knife as if I'm about to tuck in.

I sent the photograph to my father. He called me back.

'*Ciao*, Pietro!' I had a new nickname, and apparently, gender. '*Come stai?*'

He elongated the middle part the way you're supposed to, accentuating the emphasis with the quivering, jumping exclamation point that the Italians so often use instead of a question mark, turning inquiries into demands, *có·me·stài!*

He was always good at languages, accents, personas.

'*Bene, bene. Tutto bene!*'

Having exhausted the limits of our Italian we switched back to English.

'You should write about this. Write articles. My friends all think it's great, you travelling around Sicily.'

'I don't know how,' I told him, 'there are so many blogs. No one would care.'

Still, the thought lodged at the back of my mind.

Encouraged by Giuseppe, I ordered with gluttonous abandon. I wanted to try the wild boar fillet in almonds, pistachios and something called manna which he explained was a kind of sap extracted from bark. When I said I was too full for dessert I was met with sorrowful eyes. But had I ever tried a *fico d'india*? No? Well!

I must try! Giuseppe cut the pear from its cactus prickles for me at the table and it came out blushing red and tasted of water and deserts, a bit like dragon fruit, delicate and solid all at once. Why people worry about dining alone I can never understand. A table for one is a chance for improv, for connection, and if you're lucky, you'll end up with your table covered in fungi and stories.

On the way back to town, I asked the bus driver to pull over at Cala Kalura on the outskirts of Cefalù for an early evening swim to work off all that pasta. Dusk was falling and the sky deepening to a glowering smudged indigo. On the path down to the cove I passed by a house for rent with a sign advertising a *breathless view.* The beach, when I reached it, was full of small brown pebbles that glowed in the gathering twilight, and there were two iron swimming ladders set into the rocks. They always seem playful to me, making a giant pool out of the ocean.

I slipped into the water and was striking out for a rock in the distance when out of nowhere a pair of kingfishers skimmed across the waves next to me, one swooped low, then the other, metallic after metal across the darkening water. It was at times like this, when the world sharpens to a point, that I wanted so badly to share it all with my ex-boyfriend, to look with him in wonder.

'Did you see that?'

I wanted to exclaim at the birds, at the whirls of whipped cream clouds as the sun slunk low. I wanted to share all these ephemeral beauties that fall fast, almost too fast to see, but there was only me in the blue twilight water, smiling at the birds. I grew up in the countryside near a green river that cuts through the landscape of my childhood, and despite walking along its length often and always looking, I'd never seen a kingfisher before. In the cove they zipped past me so fast, so low, so unafraid to show themselves, flashing resplendent, the brightness of their oranges, the assertive fluorescences of their blues. I hadn't realised they lived by the sea, I'd thought they were only river birds.

I walked back in the rising darkness, following the coastal road to town, thinking about the flash of kingfishers and wondering what it meant.

I woke up with a start, my phone buzzing in my bed, the screen violently bright in my eyes. The UK was closing the Italian 'holiday corridor'. I blinked and sat up. I could either sprint to the airport, buy a new astronomically expensive ticket and try to get back before the deadline, or face a fortnight of solo quarantine when I returned.

Panic swirled through me, dried my mouth, pulled at my stomach like nausea. I started throwing clothes in my suitcase, sweeping an armful of cosmetics off the bathroom counter straight into the open bag, like people do in films. Shoving it closed, eyes darting around the room checking for anything left. I picked up the handle and put it down again. What was I doing?

Cutting my holiday short and rushing back to what? To be alone again, isolated again. I had known before I left this was a risk, travel corridors were opening and closing as governments fumbled. I felt hot. Needed to think. Quarantine rules meant not going outside at all, more restrictive than lockdown. Time was ticking. If I was going to leave I needed to head to the airport now.

Something clenched down hard. My body held refusal inside it, like a horse whipped to try to force it over a weakened bridge.

All at once it dawned on me that I didn't have to go anywhere. The freelance work I'd secured was fully remote. I could just stay if I wanted to. Nothing was stopping me.

But something was. What about my father? What if he caught covid or the cancer got worse? What if he was unwell and I couldn't get back? I should go. I should go now, before it was too late.

Everything felt like an emergency. Cortisol flooded through me. I needed to decide, time was ticking, but I couldn't think straight. My brain fired hot and red, lighting up and pulsing down like those MRI scans. I've never been good at decisions I can't reverse from, I always want options open, an escape route. I was between sea monsters and whirlpools.

We cling to a vine
at the cliff's edge.
There are tigers above
and below

Tigers above us and tigers below.

I called my father, staccato down the phone, talking too fast, running everything together. He listened. He said: slow down. He said: stay. I caught my breath. I paused. He explained he was going to be put on a new treatment which involved being completely isolated two weeks before and after. It was something radioactive to burst the cancer cells and he couldn't be in contact with anyone because he'd make them radioactive too. That's the thing with terminal cancer, it's not a linear thing, it depends how a person responds to the different treatments. Some cancers can be managed as a chronic condition for years with drugs 'holding the line'. So far my father had responded well to his treatments, never for quite as long as the doctors hoped, but there were always different treatment protocols to try, new drugs or different combinations.

He was between tigers too.

'But what if I need to come home?'

'You'll find a way if you have to. There'll always be a way to come home. Stay in the sunlight, Pietro, you can work from anywhere, be like one of those digital nomads.'

'What if Italy locks down?'

'You'll figure it out, you're like a cat, you land on your feet. I've always said that about you.'

I had a long, looping conversation with a calm Trailfinders travel agent who reassured me there would indeed always be a way back in case of emergency, I could come home whenever I wanted to, I'd just need to quarantine. The kind of promise I needed her to repeat to me again, like a child. I called Rachel who said to stay. I called Katharine who said to come back. I stopped myself from calling my ex-boyfriend and suddenly I was furious, this felt like his fault, leaving me to make this decision all by myself.

I left the room feeling hot. Rita took one look at me, wild-eyed, sweating panic, and made me sit down. 'Eat,' she said, and put a piece of tart in front of me. Sometimes it's that simple. I went to the beach to think, to cool down. It was windy. The sea banged relentlessly against the shore. I swam until my arms hurt. I would stay. I would swim. If regulations changed I'd figure it out. I knew I was lucky to make this choice and at the same time I also felt alone inside the instability of the world. So uncertain.

I walked back the long way from the sea to the hotel, newly appreciative of all the Italian classics – bells ringing from the churches, tiny shrines to saints at street corners, cemented in walls, on roads, in seemingly unimportant places, elevating, commemorating.

'Those old saints bless us every chance they get', there seemed to be some truth in that. Or, at least, it was a comforting thing to believe. I felt newly liberated, but on the other side of bright effervescence, darkness glinted. I knew somewhere deep inside me that facing another lockdown alone would hurt me badly, and I didn't know how long I'd be able to escape it, how the world would twist next.

For now, the road ahead stretched out, I was Kerouac. I was pretty sure it was the right call but I still felt mixed up, afraid of being locked out, afraid of not being able to get back fast enough, I was between tigers, whirlpools and sea monsters, but I was also full of a kind of lightness, something twisted tight inside me was releasing. When I called to say I was staying my father smiled. I could hear it in his voice.

'*Va bene,* Pietro,' he said, 'make the most of it.' The orange Sicilian sun filled me with optimism.

That night I slept hard, exhausted by what had felt seismic. When I woke the morning felt like the start of something new. I thought of Odysseus and his journey, he had already led me to Aeolus's islands. Something struck me and I pulled up a map on my laptop. Ithaca was nearby. I decided to travel westwards to find it.

I had become an inverse Odysseus, sailing in the other direction, away from home.

Chapter Four

A Myth is a Map

Tyrrhenian Sea

Athena, bright-eyed goddess, had a plan

On the boat I stared out to sea thinking about maps and getting lost, about imaginary islands and the places where geography and mythology collide – and whether my escape was becoming something else now, a journey, perhaps even a voyage.

I always have to turn maps round to figure out where I am, much to the disdain of my sister in law, who studied geography at Oxford. The correlation between what a map shows and what I see in the physical world is something my brain puzzles with. I am often lost, take wrong turns in every sense. When my mother names roads and rivers, I look blank, and she can't understand it because I grew up with them, but I can never seem to remember the official names of things, am never quite sure where north is, fail spatial awareness tests. The bend in the green river I love most doesn't seem to me anything like the way it's drawn on the map. The way I navigate is by landscape and memory, the remembrance of the twist of a certain road, the shape a fallen tree has made, by the things I saw and did, the people I loved. Cambridge's streets and bridges and quads are still full of ghostly signposts, so much so I can hardly bear to go back and walk past that time I broke into the gardens in one of the colleges with a boyfriend, and we kissed all night in the dark grass. The way the roses smelt that evening in the hot high summer, how young we both were.

I don't like being told what to do but I do like being shown where to go. I'm happy to follow a friend through a strange city, reliant as a child, too busy talking to remember anything about the route we took. But I could list all the addresses I've stayed in when I visit New York City, tell you coordinates about the kind of girl I was at each of those places, and how she's changed. I could give you a map to me inside cities, if you wanted it, draw my version of London for you. There'd be large swathes of vague blurry bits I never pay attention to, and then some in hyper detail – the flowers in Rachel's garden, the placement of the white metal bench at the top of the slope where we sit to watch the sun set over Greenwich, a particular tree in Victoria Park that's the best place to see the full moon, if you wanted to break in with me, squeezing through the gap in the railings late at night. I could mark the best West End streets to walk along alone if you want to feel wistful and fragile and melancholic after seeing a musical, the secret house in the East End hidden behind ivy and vines that's used for film shoots. A bench in Regent's Park where I sat, aged twenty five with a far older boyfriend, and thought I was being bohemian and daring and grown up, when in fact I was just doing exactly what he wanted me to. The pavements I've bled on, the bridges I've cried on, the cobbles on South Molton Street where I was kissed so deeply I fell in love, the flower gardens in Hyde Park where I broke up with him a year later. The street behind the Strand where I was knocked off my bike and fell in the snow, and a Jesuit priest held my hands and blessed me as my knees bled, and the snow kept falling, and the bike wouldn't work.

My father liked maps, the proper, old-fashioned paper ones. He put them in special plastic wallets that he hung around his neck on long country walks, insisted on keeping a huge yellow copy of the AA road atlas in the car at all times, years after sat nav had proved itself reliable. He could orientate with ease but had no respect for roads marked private on the map or in the world – for him that was an invitation. He loved, more than anything, to trespass, hopping the fences and gates of the grand estate near our house. I don't know why he liked it so much, as far as I knew it was one of his only transgressions. I guess to him it meant being daring, living life on the edge, wild and free. One day, walking where he shouldn't have been, he was mildly rebuked by a kindly gamekeeper, and for years afterwards muttered darkly about this man, who he christened the Baby Faced Assassin, urging me to keep a weather eye out for him when we walked together through the fields. It didn't stop him though, in all other ways a respectable, middle-class GP, in his late sixties – he called them his gangster walks.

Before there were accurate maps, there were cartographers who attempted to draw the limits of the known world, and there were also myths, which told it into being. Making a map is not just a case of technology and technique, of mathematics and spinning compasses, it's equally about aesthetics – designing and drawing an illustration of the world, folding it down into two dimensions. It's both a precise and an imaginative act. Reading a map in turn is also an imaginative act. The map-maker imagines how best to draw reality, and then we must also imagine and connect things together, to interpret it: overlaying the world of the map onto what we see in front of us. I like to draw on maps, mark where I've been, sketch out my hiking routes in pen after I've completed them, draw in black the path I took to get to the mountain.

At the edges of their maps, where the cartographers had no more information, story took over, carving terrible monsters in strange lands, making sea creatures into mermaids, foretelling of danger and doom, of valour and courage. Stories tell us the contours of the world in more dimensions and more colours than Ordnance Survey could ever capture. Myths create meaning, show us how to find our way when we're lost and alone and not feeling in the least bit brave. They give us heroines and allies and perils and the ever-burnished hope of redemption, of finding our way home again, and being welcomed back, at long last. Science can't tell us about death and afterwards, but stories can.

Myths are also our earliest, oldest geography lessons, explaining the shape of the world. Storms and tempests and exploding volcanos are the unpredictable wrath of gods. Way before meteorologists poured sunshine into mathematical equations so they could forecast the weather, the Greeks invented Helius. Whether he would shine tomorrow was immeasurable, dependent on his mood as he gunned his fire-chariot across the sky. When ships were lost at sea, someone had forgotten to venerate Poseidon, and even if they had made a sacrifice to him, deaths at sea could still be explained since the god of the ocean, like all the rest, held grudges, was petty.

Myths can also be mapped – the link between imaginary and real places has obsessed people over the centuries seeking to understand where *The Odyssey* was set, where Ithaca was located, pondering which islands best correlate to the descriptions of the fantastical lands given in the story. Emily Wilson's view is pragmatic – she says, 'there is some correspondence between the world of Homer and the real world, although the relationship is partial and inexact'. Partial and inexact have not deterred generations of scholars from putting competing theories forward, often based on nothing much more than speculation and whimsy.

It started with ancient scholars like Strabo, the godfather of geography. Then in the nineteenth century, due to the revival of classical studies and the surge in travel and exploration, there was an explosion of interest in trying to figure out where precisely the mythical lands of *The Odyssey* were, in real world geography. Scholars pored over descriptions in the story, the placement of a cave, the arrangement of the stars, and how geological forms were rendered in the poem, to try and figure out the correspondence to actual islands. There's no real consensus and the theories diverge and morph. Some are hyper specific: for example, that the Strait of Messina with its tricky currents is exactly where Odysseus got trapped between the whirlpool and the sea monster, while others talk more broadly – about the coastline of southern Italy being an inspiration for the fantastical lands, rather than an exact rendering.

Something about this attempt to map the imaginary onto concrete-literal geography, its futile nature perhaps, caught my attention and held it. I have a propensity to spin into story, to fill in the gaps with what I want to believe, to tell myself wild romance or deep tragedy, even when the cold data might suggest otherwise. If myths function to help us make meaning of the world, maps help us find our footing, understand where we are in gravitational space. I needed both.

I pictured those nineteenth-century men, smoking their pipes, stabbing their fingers at passages in the poem, arguing with each other, earnestly defending their theories. The gap between all their different maps was what fascinated me most, it opened up space for multiple interpretations. In this strange, upside-down world, their mapping projects made a mad kind of sense to me. With peril and fear all around, I needed a different map, a way to access the mythical, to believe in the gods again. Perhaps I would find my island home by following Odysseus to his.

As a lonely child, I was schooled early in the powers of the imagination to transcend – books opened worlds, let me travel. Prose and logic is all well and good but give me poetry too, give me romance and stories, tell me how a nymph cried so hard for her lover that her tears became a cold, clear river in Sicily where women wash clothes, how the volcano is an irascible mountain god (the patriarchy, even in symbolic form, is never satisfied), not just tectonic plates slowly bumping around deep under water. Show me how whales sing melancholic operas about the poisoning of the oceans, chanting a litany for the world. When I'm stung by jellyfish, remind me that octopuses eat them, and that an octopus has three hearts and blue blood. Call my attention by ringing silvery bells in small Italian towns at odd hours, chiming through the air saying look and look and look.

The world was uncertain, it was impossible to chart a course. I had to trust to the fates. Odysseus was emerging as a mirror, my twin, both of us running from horror – Troy for him and heartbreak and an unwell father inside a pandemic for me. Following Odysseus's journey was starting to become an anchor to hold on to in an unsettling world, a sort of guiding force giving shape to my travels, making sense out of chaos. But while his goal was fixed and certain – to get home – mine was more amorphous: to stay away.

I was pulled from these thoughts by sea spray flicking across the windows. The boat was bouncing roughly over the waves now as we sailed closer to the island, green coming into focus against the blue. A bag fell from the luggage rack behind me and a dog started barking frantically. I wanted to slip from the brutality of the real world contaminated by fear, away from its pain and horror, its hysteria and invisible pathogens, its cancer and covid, into the 'wine-dark sea' where Odysseus's ship rocks in the waves, where gods tantrum and sea monsters lurk. I wanted to move through all my spirals of regret and the weight of the past, away from knowing how slender my foundations were, how easily unmoored I could be. I wanted to be held inside story, to suspend disbelief and watch

Dawn awaken the sky in disco colours, pink and yellow and orange, bright with possibility.

There was no map to this pandemic, we were at the edges of the known world, doing our best to navigate our different ways through it. Whatever I was doing now seemed to be unfolding into something else and I didn't have a word for it, just a weird ancient poem and a half-formed plan to follow it and find the places where imaginary lands and the real world came together. It was only later that I realised it had become a compass.

The boat swayed as it pulled into the port and I stumbled as I walked down the gangway on to Marettimo, wondering if I would find Ithaca here.

Chapter Five

Sunny Ithaca

Marettimo, Egadi archipelago, Sicily, Italy

my Ithaca is set apart, most distant,
facing the dark. It is a rugged land

Odysseus

Marettimo translates as 'sea thyme'. The island's namesake scented the air but there was something else in the atmosphere too. When I arrived it was overcast and there was a mysterious feel about the place, bordering on ominous. The boat pulled into the harbour outside the main fishing village which looked slightly Greek, with boxy white houses and light blue shutters. I walked up the mostly empty streets in search of coffee. The few locals I met were broadly uninterested, entirely lacking in the usual Sicilian charm. The islanders here are known for their obstinacy and dislike of tourists. Not surprising, perhaps, given Marettimo is remote, lying forty-five kilometres off the western coast of Sicily – the furthest of the islands in the Egadi archipelago, it has a reputation for being a rough, piratical place, full of mountains and birds and beauty but hard and unforgiving too. The population is small and there are no cars on the island, everything is too vertical. Eventually I found a bar, the kind of place dominated by fluorescent strip lighting, a screaming television, and a few morose people smoking heavily outside. I loaded my *espresso lungo* with sugar and drank it fast.

Samuel Butler believed this place was Ithaca, Odysseus's home. An English novelist who became famous for writing satires about Victorian society, he'd gone to New Zealand to escape his religious father and make his fortune, and on his return to England, produced a translation of *The Odyssey*. The effort, apparently, was trivial. 'The Greek being easy, I had little difficulty in understanding what I read'. Furthermore, because he was not a Greek scholar, and therefore came to the text with 'fresh eyes', Butler discovered what others had completely missed: Ithaca was not in Greece, and Homer had been misgendered.

To him, it was blindingly obvious the poem was the work of a 'brilliant, high spirited woman' and that when this 'poetess' wrote about Ithaca she was picturing the island of Marettimo. This belief, the lack of any actual evidence for it, or possibly the arrogant terms in which it was expressed, greatly annoyed his contemporaries. In his book *The Authoress of the Odyssey* Samuel also claimed that the 'poetess' had written herself into the story as the character of Nausicaa, a young, beautiful princess that naked Odysseus has to beg for clothes after being shipwrecked. All slightly awkward, but Nausicaa is composed, and barely bats an eyelid when she's confronted by the grubby nudist. Might this be the first feminist retelling of Greek mythology? Emily Wilson says it's pretty unlikely, 'we have, sadly, no evidence for women participating in the archaic Greek epic tradition as composers', and she suggests moreover that Samuel's theory is actually fairly insulting, since he attributes what he regards as the clunky elements of the poem to it being written by a young, unmarried girl.

The idea of 'home' is incredibly powerful in the poem, returning home is the singular animating force sustaining Odysseus through all his challenges. What is a home? It's obviously more than a physical house, a familiar place, a beloved landscape. It seems to me that home is an imaginative expectation of acceptance, belonging, of being truly known and loved. There's an idealised romance contained inside those four letters, an embrace inside the words 'welcome home' which perhaps can never be fully realised – we can't all come back to fatted calves. But if this island was 'sunny Ithaca' to Samuel, it didn't feel particularly welcoming to me.

My plan was to hike across the island following the coastal trail from the scruffy village over to Punta Troia, a castle on the northern shore set on a peninsula which curled out like a dragon's tail. I wanted to get a feel for the place and to stretch out my legs again after several days sitting still at my desk, making a start on my new freelance work, and then a day in transit to get here from Cefalù, including a night at Trapani, the port city on the western coast. I needed to figure out a plan and walking always helps me think more clearly. Thoughts slot together better in my mind when I'm in motion. It feels like as my body works, so my mind becomes fluid. I was looking for somewhere to make my temporary home and it made sense to start with the island that was supposedly Ithaca.

Autumn had started to colour the plants along the trail in different shades of fire, although there was plenty of green here still. Turning inland, the path wound through scrubby woodland with so many birds flying through it that it felt like Snow White's forest. The place is famous among birdwatchers and botanists and I could see why. At the end of the wood was a plain wooden sign pointing up a slope to *sorgente*, which my phone translated mysteriously as 'the source'.

I followed the detour up a hill and discovered a miniature grotto deep in the woods. Inside there was a small statue of outstretched, ever forgiving Mary in a pale variation of her usual outfit: white dress, light-blue robes, with an especially mild and content expression on her face. Her eyes were lowered as she stared down into the pool at her reflection. The opposite of Narcissus, ironically adopting his pose. She was draped in an oversized rosary and behind her was 'the source', a freshwater stream that dripped softly onto green moss and then ran into a shallow stone trough carved into the rock below. It felt like a child's fairy house in the woods but with the holy mother for a toy. There was a sense of peace here or maybe it was Mary's presence. The only sound was the irregular, gently dripping water, and the wind weaving through the trees. The green of the moss and the plants growing from the rock walls around the cave was startlingly bright. I sat for a while and cupped my hands to drink the blessed water, took one swallow and started worrying I might pick up some kind of amoeba.

I retraced my steps back to the main path and after the wood the landscape turned empty, a yellow coastal trail cutting through low plants decked out in matching shades of yellow, contrasting against the sea blue. Eventually, the path became a slope of loose black scree leading downhill, slippery and difficult to walk on. I tripped and fell, I wasn't wearing proper hiking boots, wasn't paying attention, going too fast like always. I flicked away the grit and sucked the blood from the gashes on my hand, rotated my ankle tentatively, got up and almost immediately fell down again. At least there was no one to see me. In front of me, Castello di Punta Troia rose up at the top of a hill on its own thin promontory, and the sea shook up against either side of the causeway. From where I was, I could see the winding path to the top visibly carved into the barren hill in front of me. When I got up there, the castle itself was small and boxy, a series of squares rising up from a stone tower. It had been restored and a sign informed me it was now a prison museum and monk seal observatory.

The second I reached the doorway, panting, thirsty and lightly bleeding, two guides bounded over and enthusiastically offered me a free tour of the castle. The island was empty of all tourists, I could barely even buy a coffee and yet this remote *castello* miles away from anywhere was open and fully staffed. If Italy beguiles, Sicily bewilders.

The younger guide, Vittorio, a teenager in a black tracksuit, was still a boy but smiled the easy, confident smile of Italian men. The castle, he told me, used to be a watchtower but became a prison in 1793. He opened a trapdoor and showed me some dark steps down into 'the cave' but forbade me to descend. We looked together into the darkness.

'They went to the toilet in this cave. In the whole, fifty-two prisoners live in here. Life is totally in the cave. Eat, drink, all in the cave. In the pit, twenty types of insects. Very wild conditions.'

Vittorio smiled encouragingly at me, as if being kept in a dark pit wasn't bad enough, it was important that I understood the prisoners were additionally tormented by many different insects.

'Did they die in there or did they come out?'

'No. Not died!'

It seemed highly unlikely that no one had ever died here but Vittorio's English was limited and my Italian was far worse. Theo was obsessed with prisons, I think it was living through lockdown, so I took some photographs to show him, and we left it there, on an optimistic note.

A white goat bounced down the sheer cliff. The waters below the castle curled and crested in their whites and blues. Vittorio told me he saw dolphins from here, and monk seals and whales.

At the end of the tour he presented me with a selection of postcards of jellyfish for a reason I couldn't quite catch. I hitched a lift back on the water taxi that came to collect the guides and as the boat chopped through the water I turned the cards over in my hands. They were advertising an EU 'counter mitigation' project on jellyfish. Due to climate change, 'blooms' of jellyfish had increased, and two million bathers were stung every year, the cards informed me solemnly, and in the strangely choked language of policy said this 'proliferation represents a growing threat for human and coastal activities'. As one of the two million, I was happy to know that action was being taken against my enemies. I texted my friend Katharine a picture of the postcards – *my enemies have enemies,* I wrote. She texted back the skull emoji, the jellyfish emoji and the snake emoji.

ENCHANTED ISLANDS

Back in the village, I met Salvatore, a jeweller in his forties who wore a flat cap, smoked roll-ups and had a wide, brilliant smile. He told me the legend behind the castle. A prince lived here because there's always a prince, and two sisters were in love with him because girls get like that around princes. He was in love with one sister and one day the unloved sister happened to be in the palace and told the loved sister that the prince had switched his love to her. The loved sister at once committed bloody suicide right then and there because what is the point of living if you're an unloved woman. The unloved sister confessed her lie to the prince. Running to the crumpled, bloodied body of his beloved, the angry prince attempted to hurl the unloved sister out of the castle window to die in the sea, but she clung on to him and clawed him down with her so they both drowned.

'So, everybody died?'

'*Sì*, everyone died.'

'That's a horrible story,' I said to Salvatore.

'That's what our legends are like in Sicily, all very tragic, all very sad,' he said, grinning.

The symbolism did not escape me, an ancient castle, tragic love stories, a prison with twenty insects. There was something circular about it, a message about leaving and returning. This was not a place for me to stay. Marettimo may have been Ithaca for Butler but it felt more hostile than homelike to me. Or perhaps it was me feeling strange and projecting this on to the landscape. After all, the idea of home raises expectations that it often cannot meet. Home is synonymous with safety but my home in London was riven now with danger. Returning to my childhood house also wasn't an option because of my father's obsessive caution about covid. When home is no longer safe you can leave, if you're lucky, or be exiled if you're not, like Rosselli on Lipari. Islands can be both paradise and prison. I felt a new awareness of everything I'd taken for granted, a home, security: I had a place to go back to if I wanted. I thought of all the people forced to flee their homes for terrible reasons, for war, I thought of the displaced, those who never had homes, and those who had lost them.

Maybe home is more of a feeling, a place where you feel settled, and if that's the case, there can be many ways to form different homes through the world. But it's also about heart, about people. I'd never planned to live alone and, although I'm self-reliant, I've never been the slightest bit self-contained. I'm high on the extroversion scale, meaning I like people around me all the time, and look more outwards than inwards. Before lockdown I was only ever a conversation away from connection and possibility.

As I waited by the port I thought again of those tigers above and below, the new sharpness of the world, its breathtaking brutality and its unexpected softness. 'Tigers swim,' Theo had told me with the delight children have in new facts they've just learned, on our most recent video call. He was a rainbow tiger, he said, and he had two new imaginary friends, one good, one reprehensible. His alliances changed between them daily.

After many adventures in the 'salt sea' Odysseus winds up on an island where the Phaeacians live, a people famous for their sailing and dancing. They offer him accommodation and a chance to rest, and even organise a sports day to cheer him up when he bursts into tears at dinner. They end up giving him a magical self-steering ship which is how he finally gets back home to Ithaca in the end.

I wasn't interested in going back home yet, even if someone gave me a magical ship, but I didn't want to stay here either. I shivered and looked to the dark horizon for the last boat to Favignana, reputed to be the island of goats and wonders in *The Odyssey*.

As you set out for Ithaka
hope your road is a long one,
full of adventure, full of discovery.

Chapter Six

Enchanted Island

Favignana, Egadi archipelago, Sicily, Italy

When early Dawn shone forth with rosy fingers,
we roamed around that island full of wonders

Odysseus

I rode into birdsong, into colour, the light doing its beautiful golden Hollywood thing, glimmering against the white rocks on the low stone walls. The ease of it felt like I was cheating – life flowed. There was a spaciousness as I cycled, a lateral stretching of soundscape, big skies, birds fluting. I didn't meet anyone else on the narrow lanes and had a sense of being completely alone on an island of two thousand. The bike crunched on the sand in the rutted lanes and juddered into potholes making my bag and water bottle jump in the basket. Is there anything happier than being on a bicycle early in the morning heading to the sea?

I was cycling through the rising dawn across Favignana for a morning dip. The spinning sound of my wheels whirred metallic, a dog barked in the distance, a cockerel shrieked in outrage at the unstoppable rise of the sun. Paused. Repeated himself: the masculine imperative to be listened to, a demanding entitlement to attention. The quiet was stretched full of conversational bird I couldn't translate well enough to distinguish the different songs and melodies, the same way I couldn't understand Sicilian. Instead I just heard it collectively, simplified, a generalised calling to joy.

I had woken, like I woke here each day, at six, springing lightly out of bed, the way I never could in London, where unsticking myself from warmth in the cold grey seemed almost impossible, where alarms went unanswered and good intentions were buried under pillows and eye masks and earplugs that shut out the gritty noise, the watery charcoal light. Here I was transformed, finally what I hoped to become – a virtuous person. The type of girl who's an effortless early riser, who extols daily attendance of the dawn chorus, one of those smug people who elongates the day by getting up with the light, and claims never to be tired. In the before-ness of the day opening fully I seemed to achieve things with ease, writing in my journal before my morning coffee, cycling and swimming before I had to sit still at my desk. I was self-satisfied, content, no longer at war with myself for trying and failing, not castigating my own laziness. I was better here. I lived better. I checked the wind on the app on my phone, selected a cove in the opposite direction to minimise the chance of jellyfish stings, pulled on warm trousers and hopped on my *bici* as the sky pinked and blushed.

The weather was cooling into autumn now and the sea was noticeably colder. Every day at the shore I fought myself. I knew I'd feel better after I plunged, but still I hesitated. Wasted long moments each morning standing with water up to my thighs, my legs turning white, my soft stomach flinching from the cold sting. I have always liked the aesthetic of discipline, its boundedness. I see the pleasure in deprivation, frugality, I grew up with the austere Catholic kind of strictness: punishment, self-denial, guilt. Sometimes I practised intermittent fasting in London, using the hunger to sharpen productivity and concentration, but this swimming practice was more than just discipline. It was equal parts exploding, endorphinic pleasure. When I did finally get in and felt my breath catch and release, felt the cold move across and into me, there was a brutality to it at first, then it deepened into peacefulness and finally joy as my body braced and then relaxed and delighted. I was grinning like an idiot as I shook into my clothes and pedalled back fast on numbed, clawed feet, trying to warm up.

My newfound ability to get up early, combined with the one hour time difference between here and England, expanded the mornings into something languid, something owned, before I had to put my head into my laptop and solve problems like puzzles, write down my findings, map evidence, make recommendations. The work, too, felt easier and more contained, my usual restlessness had been channelled by the cycling and swimming, my focus, my attention improved.

After about a week on the island I had become an accepted part of the daily crowd at Bar Cono, the *caffè* on the corner of the square. This was where all the old boys took coffee but they knew me by now and chattered at me in fast Italian, asking where I'd been swimming today, opining on the best cove for me to try tomorrow, warning me of *mare brutto* (ugly sea), shaking their heads over the eccentric English girl in glasses and straw hat who liked *acqua fredda* (cold water). We had long conversations even though all I ever did was nod and say '*sì, sì*', clenching my hands into fists and opening them over and over to help my fingers re-pink from the ghost yellow they'd turned in the water. It turns out that agreeableness is all anyone really wants from a conversational partner. I was more amenable, less acerbic in translation. I smiled more too, to compensate for my limitations, my lack of Italian, and also because I was happy again. It had been rising through me like smoke, sweetly gentle and light, so that at first I didn't notice, the way a cat crawls on top when you're sleeping and you only realise when it springs off in the morning, or the way a fever crescendos and catches then breaks deep in the mid of night but you're too sick or sleepy to notice you're better until the next day, and you realise it, backwards.

We sat on the *terrazza* in the fresh air, buying each other espressos, watching people queuing at the bakery across the *piazza* or cycling through the square. I loved that I was greeted by name, I loved that I was known, that in a way I belonged.

'*Ciao*, Lao-ra! *Caffè?*'

I nodded my head, insisted it was my turn to pay, and poured *zucchero de canna* into my tiny china cup. Unthinkable to sweeten my coffee at home. Unthinkable for my father to ever drink coffee from a mug, he always insisted on a proper cup and saucer – in that way he was just a little bit out of time. *La dolce vita*, I thought as I stirred the sugar into my espresso, is very literally correct, Italy was fat-full of sweetness.

'This is your home now,' said Maria, her painted red lips staining the end of the white cigarette she was using as a pointer to show me around the hotel. I had persuaded her to keep it open just for me. There were no other customers and I could stay as long as I liked. A whole hotel to live in as a long-term resident, there was something old Hollywood about it. I don't play princess much but I immediately took custody of the 'Princessa' room and felt like a queen in her palace. There was a fancy shower in a cubicle slightly too small for the rainfall effect to work properly, and a large roof terrace edged around with glass, which felt luxurious. This was where I moved through the pendulum of my yoga practice each evening after my second swim, where I watched the moon glow at night and the stars sparkle through the sky. Barefoot, my frozen white toes slowly turning pink again on my black mat as the night deepened into darkness. Yellow street lights started to shine across the scruffy white village, cats called with feline sex in their voices, the church shook its bells at unbelievers, the green mountain turned charcoal and became just an outline, and behind it all, there was the swish of the sea as evening fell.

It felt imaginary, this island, like something dreamed. Monte Santa Catarina with its romantically slumped castle, rocky coves for swimming, a tiger striped sea, tough Sicilian locals instead of the usual fawning service you get in seaside summery places. Light flowed liquid, bright blue skies above the yellow church with its three brass bells. Shrines to saints everywhere I looked – cemented into low stone walls, on the corners of streets, next to shop windows, flowers in vases honouring them. Peregrine falcons lived on the mountainside and vibrated incognito, hovering over fields in their moth-brown plumage, making my heart jump every time I spotted them as I rode past.

To me it felt exactly how islands should feel. Not once could I forget I was entirely surrounded by water, the sea surged and pulled at the shore wherever I went. In New York City I had developed a habit of walking laterally across town, from water to water. I did this every time I visited, and still Manhattan never felt island-ish to me, even though I knew it was, even though I'd walked its watery boundedness. In England it's impossible for me to consider that I'm on an island. The dirty, grey, truculent English seaside is too far away from almost everyone, there is no sense of buoyancy. It had felt like there was something huge and broken in the centre of London before I left. Or perhaps it was just me that didn't belong there any more.

Slow and easy. A parallel world. An island off an island off Italy. An exercise in small-scale living, in sufficiency. There was enough of everything here but not too much of anything. I cycled over the *chiuso* (closed) old mountain road, strictly forbidden to all traffic ever since a tunnel was carved through Monte Santa Catarina, but in the Italian style, everyone just lifted their bikes over the barriers because it was far more beautiful to ride along the old road with the sea yawning along on your left, with cactuses clinging to the mountain slopes and pink and purple wildflowers along the edges.

I had found a hidden beach across a field on the other side of the mountain, and Cala Pirreca became one of my favourite places. I sat in the shade of a cave in the cliff as the sea played with pebbles on the beach. The wind was right so I swam out to Isola Preveto, a rocky island about half a kilometre off the shore. It was a seductively easy swim on the way out and I always forgot how dicey the currents on the return were. On the outbound leg I pulled myself up the rocks to rest and warm up, but never stayed for long because someone had told me the island was exclusively inhabited by 'the so big mouses'. It took me a beat to realise what they meant.

Not a single car beeped at me when I cycled here, unlike London where being on a bicycle meant being sworn at daily. Predictable and grinding. Here I was relaxed, my shoulders freckling as I moved on my *bicicletta* through the thick quietness on the island, the texture of peace.

I cycled along the west coast to the monochrome lighthouse where shallow rock pools had formed from the exoskeleton of an old quarry and swam. As I sat drying on the rocks, two kingfishers zipped past electric, skimming the water, one flying so close to my knee I felt the vibrations of the wing-beaten wind. Their flash was like a rent in the world, a glimpse of another realm. It was the second time kingfishers had come to me, again moving so fast I wasn't quite sure if I'd seen or imagined them. A blue-orange blur, a whipping flight, a conjuring trick.

Ernie Bradford, an English historian and antiques enthusiast, published a book called *Ulysses Found* in the sixties. In it he suggested that Favignana was the island of goats, or in Emily's translation the 'island full of wonders', that Odysseus and his crew stopped at before they went to confront the Cyclops. In the story Zeus's daughters drive the mountain goats towards them, so the hunting is good, and the men enjoy a proper Sicilian feast:

> ... *we sat there*
> *all day till sunset, eating meat and drinking*
> *our strong red wine*

But for me Favignana felt more like Circe's island, a place of magical enchantments, than somewhere to hunt goats – in all my time I never saw a single one here. All the geographical theories seemed pretty subjective to me, so why not invent my own? In the story, Circe is a powerful sorceress and turns the crew into pigs. Odysseus, guided by Hermes, manages to outwit her, by eating a protective herb that means her magic won't work on him, convinces her to change his men back, and then sleeps with her (of course). I was the enchantress, the witch, the goddess, the goat. This was my wild island and anything could happen.

It was a clear blue evening and I was pacing around the roof terrace looking at the dome of the church, at the roofs of the old houses, as I spoke to my father.

'How are you? Been for another long run?' I asked. He laughed and I heard something catching in his breath, the same way you can see vapour in cold air on Christmas walks. Something new. A hint of an effort to breathe.

I looked up at the full moon, at its fat glossiness, at the rabbit I saw in its shadows, trying to un-hear this change. Noticing these things felt like another betrayal.

'Oh yes, I'm training for the marathon,' he said, and again I heard that slight strain, a whisper of it, perhaps it meant this latest treatment was working, wrecking its way through his body on its mission to blast the cancer cells.

'For an Iron Man, don't you mean? About to have a pureed chicken protein shake?'

'Yes, I'm just about to have my chicken infusion.'

'What's that?'

'A rectal infusion of chicken.' We fenced and danced in conversations designed to amuse, sometimes drawing blood. We played hard the way we always played. Neither of us would soften, would do anything differently. Neither of us would suddenly turn saccharine, too sweet. This is how you show love sometimes, pretending everything is normal. He had asked me once, right at the start, when he got his diagnosis, not to suffocate him with compassion. I would keep my word. My eyes went hot and started to vibrate but I kept steady, blinking up at the yellow moon until the water reabsorbed, not letting it fall.

He had actually run the London marathon once, back when he was well, and to commemorate, blew up two massive photographs of himself wearing a green t-shirt and his faithful bumbag, both arms outreached as if he was already over the finish line, an anticipatory victory pose. He put one of them right by his desk, lest he forgot his own accomplishments, and one immediately opposite the main door of the house, to prompt visitors to ask about it. He was a vain man, he liked to boast, not just about himself, but also about me. Sometimes I worried I hadn't given him much material compared to my brother.

––––––––

Clemente, one of the old fishermen I drank coffee with at the bar, handed me his business card one day, advertising boat tours. On the back was a photograph taken years earlier: a huge tuna fish being hauled onto a boat by five men, all of them leaning right back and grimacing with the effort, the giant fish with five wooden harpoons sticking out of its stomach, and its fin pointing upwards, as if at god. Clemente pointed at the man with blonde hair and then at himself, making sure I understood.

I had noticed the old tuna factory, at one end of the harbour. It was a series of elegant buildings and long boathouses with orange-tiled roofs, five tall red-brick chimneys pointing up towards the mountain, and a high wall all around it. There were four huge archways opening directly on to the water, for launching boats I guessed. I'd vaguely realised there was some kind of tuna connection with the island from the many graphic portrayals of bloodied fishing on the tiles and pictures in the shops around the village, but now looking at Clemente's business card, I wanted to understand the history properly.

I was the only one on the group tour. Anna, the guide, told me that at one point in the fifteenth century the island belonged to someone who called himself 'The Baron of Tuna', on account of the bluefins that thicken the waters here because the island is bang on their migration paths. However, it was when Favignana was sold to Ignazio Florio in the nineteenth century that things got seriously bad for the tuna fish. The Florio family built the largest factory in the Mediterranean and invented ever more cruel and ingenious ways to trap the fish, culminating in a sadistic system of seven underwater nets leading to the 'death room' where the tuna either killed each other with the thrashing of their tails, or were harpooned to death. These *tonnare* nets were so large it took the whole of April to set them up, ready for the season which began in May.

Once caught, the fish were hung from their tails before being cooked and canned in astonishing numbers. Even the cans were extraordinary. The biggest I'd ever seen, huge tub-like cans for the army, the size of a hug. Everything was vertically integrated, the cans were also made in this factory, and the boats used to fish the tuna were constructed across the harbour at the shipyard opposite. According to Anna even the idea of adding keys to open the can, and the system of preserving the tuna in oil inside the can, were both invented here. No part of the tuna was wasted, oil was made from boiling the heads of the fish and the bones were crunched into fertiliser. Cresting each can was a lion, the symbol of the Florios, it was kneeling on one paw, tongue out lapping at a puddle. Apparently, the lion was drinking quinine to cure himself from malaria, a tribute to the family's pharmacy business. Florio lions are carved into the factory doors here and can also be found all over the finest churches in Palermo. The factory closed its doors in 1982 but tuna continued to be fished in the traditional way, using the long wooden harpoons, until as recently as 2007.

When I was a child my brain correlated the size of the tuna can with the size of the fish, so for years I thought they were like sardines or anchovies. It was only at university watching a nature documentary that I realised the truth. Looking at these tuna cans was instructive, I was reminded of the short circuits of my own thought processes, my assumptions, how stupid I can be.

Sometimes being ignorant is a good thing. On the island I was safe in more ways than just physically. I was insulated by the language barrier. Anxiety couldn't spiral because I could no more understand the fear and worries of the people chatting in the square than I could distinguish the different calls of the birds. To me everything was song. Italian sounds to me like bubbles or cats singing, and Sicilian, with its blurred 's' notes, is earthier, more sibilant, holding just a hint of menace in its hushing consonants. It was a relief to be ignorant, to speak only my basic needs like a child, to not be burdened with expectations of being articulate or amusing. I had only to smile or shrug, and even my shrugs became more dramatic in this land of pantomime gesticulation, they now included the corners of my mouth pulled down, as well as my shoulders and arms. My basic attempts at speaking the language were encouraged with enormous affection, with affirmation and smiles, the way you cheer on a small baby learning to crawl or stand.

My favourite gesture was when Sicilians hold both hands loosely just below their sternum in a kind of horizontal prayer and then shake it up and down mournfully. *Non posso faci nulla*, they are saying (I can't do anything about it). It is a gesture of acceptance and surrender and a negotiation technique too. Sliding three fingers up the throat and flicking them fast from the chin means decisive indifference: *non me va* (I don't care), whereas holding fingertips together with thumbs like upturned baby beaks and oscillating them in the air means alternatively *cosa vuoi* (what do you want?) or *che ci posso fare* (what can I do?). Sign language helped me follow along.

Occasionally, I pretended to share the sorrow people expressed about my *non parlo italiano* and made empty promises to learn. Some words caught, because they sounded pretty: *brioches con tuppe* meant they have 'little hats', *zenzero* is the flashy word for ginger, and every time I asked for *latte schiuma* the word made me feel light and frothy. I was happy in my bubble, skimming along.

I've always loved language, words, lexicon, the ability to say one thing in different ways, to try and catch something between the letters in sentences, never thought that the absence of it could be seductive. Previously when I'd travelled, I felt the language barrier only as something frustrating, a wall to hurl myself against, revealing the embarrassing inadequacies of my education. I would write down words and numbers as I tried to learn Spanish when I roamed around Colombia, practising with people on buses, but here it was more balm than barrier. It was like being inside a bubble wrap envelope in the post, or like sitting in the back seat of a car driven at night by your parents, watching the cat's eyes in the road reflect green, the street lights flashing by yellow, tired and big-eyed in the dark, having childish grand thoughts about the city lights looking like the inverted spots of a leopard. I was choosing not to know, couldn't participate in collective worry about the pandemic's latest movements, in the hysterical micro interpretations, in macro conspiracies. I didn't have to deal with banal observations about the world, petty complaints, whinging. Not knowing what anyone was really saying, I could choose to believe the old fishermen were having elevated conversations about art and poetry each morning.

I also knew that I was choosing not to know about my father. At the very beginning, when he was diagnosed, years ago, mistaking my optimism, my hopefulness, for denial, he tried to ram it home as we stood on the street outside my brother's house in London.

'I'm afraid your old dad won't make old bones.'

I nodded, to show I understood. He hated shows of emotion and I couldn't trust my voice.

'I want you to act normal,' he said.

It was sharp, an order, not the extraction of a promise. This was when he told me not to suffocate him with compassion. So I knew what not to do but I was still uncertain about what to do. I hugged him then. It was weird. Hugging was something we never did, it was something I'd watched my friends doing with their fathers, feeling strange and envious about it, something that happened in the movies.

Then there was a handbrake turn. The doctors had diagnosed stomach cancer originally. As a doctor himself, he was puzzled. The risk factors weren't there, it didn't make sense, and yet there it was, a grey mass in the stomach, large and revolting, an upside down cow's udder. Three to six months. We braced. A half-life or a doubling of time, an absurdity of an estimate. But soon the diagnosis flicked on to something else. A different type, neuroendocrine, a slower growing cancer, one that was operable.

'Not containable because it has fled the nest,' he told me. It had metastasised, an ugly word. 'The ones in the liver are what will get me in the end,' he said, his own organ a stealth weapon of mass destruction. Still, there was much more time after they reversed the diagnosis and if an operation and drugs could control it, there might be years.

I raged at the wasted emotions of the doctors getting it wrong. How could they sit across from a person and say they have three months to live and then say, sorry, I made a mistake, actually it's this totally other kind of cancer? Because he was medical he didn't think like that. These things happen. It was good news. He was lucky. And psychologically I think it was better this way for him, in the end. Going from worse to bad makes it easier to feel grateful.

On the island I stilled my mind with cold water, froze my thoughts, wove my body in and out of contorted shapes and difficult balances in yoga poses which required all my concentration, wobbling on one leg, staring at one point. These things helped me, wouldn't let me think about him, the pandemic, whether I had wasted my life. These things were scaffolding. Flipping from a headstand into a wheel I couldn't feel anything other than breath and muscles stretching and movement, were my legs engaged enough? Were my shoulders lifted to support my neck? I could move inside my own physiology, deep in the body, away from the heat of my mind – 'bio-hacking', those exhausting tech bros would call it – drugging myself with water, artificially forcing endorphins, dopamine hits. My muscles curved, I could track the strength in my handstands: I was getting better at holding myself the wrong way up. After each day I was physically sore and tired enough to sleep too deep to dream. I knew what I was doing. I knew I was moving the anxiety into motion. And I knew if I stopped, if I sat still, what might happen.

In *The Odyssey* libations are frequently offered to the gods as part of elaborate rituals. Wine is poured into the ground as prayers are said, asking for favour, for protection, to get home safely. Animals are sacrificed and burned down to the bones as gifts, but the offerings don't always work. The gods are not easily pleased, nor are their tempers always assuaged.

I had taken to making my own offerings, sea pebbles, stacked stones, sea glass thrown to the waves, a way of giving thanks for being here in this magical place. I offered libations to the old gods in the ancient way, and asked for more time, but my tributes were too small and the gods were silent and I knew in a small way what I did not want to know.

I was in a shop near the old boat factory when I met Alice. Except she wasn't Alice the same way I was no longer Laura. She was Ahleechay and I was Lao-ra. She was slim and poised with elegant clothes, short grey hair and the kind of mouth that has a propensity to smile.

'I feel like I'm the last tourist in town,' I said, gesturing to the empty shop.

'You're not quite,' she said, 'but almost.'

I looked at all the things for sale, buying nothing, while she told me her uncle had a hotel 'on the other side of the island' on the secluded west coast, past the tunnel that bisected the mountain. There was an olive farm too, and they kept bees and donkeys.

'It sounds beautiful,' I said.

'I would like to propose you to come for breakfast tomorrow. Come as my guest.'

There were handsome brown donkeys in the fields and yellow flowers along the verges as I piloted the *bici* down the bumpy tracks early the next morning. Alice's hotel was grand and quiet and beautiful. The tables were set in the garden and she offered me warm ricotta cheese from a local shepherd drizzled with thyme honey from their bees. It was like eating clouds and the honey tasted almost medicinal. Alice's theory was that because the island is dry and flowers here survive with very little water this concentrates their scent, in turn giving the honey extra flavour. 'The same way that the best tomatoes in Sicily grow with no water, just taking humidity from the air. Next, I propose you scrambled eggs with fresh mint,' she said, 'and after that there's a selection of home-made cakes.' A 'selection' was an understatement, there were enough kinds of cake to make Marie Antoinette happy, and the mint in the eggs was a revelation.

After I was finished with my investments in gout and girth, Alice showed me around the rooms, with outside bathtubs in cactus gardens, with a view across to Marettimo over in the west, and my favourite, a high room, reached by an outside staircase, where the bed was dressed in soft pinks and whites, and there were lanterns on the terrace. It looked like love and romance and it panged into me, how much I wanted someone to be alongside me here, how I missed the ease and easiness of being a couple, wanting to sit with my ex-boyfriend on the terrace and watch the sun set behind blue Marettimo across the sea.

Before covid stopped him in his tracks, my father was always in the world, always gathering new people to him. More than anything he liked to meet strangers, delighted in getting to know and interrogating my friends, although this sometimes backfired. When he saw an old flatmate of mine he hadn't seen for a couple of years, he clocked her changed appearance. She had broken up with her boyfriend, cut her hair, got fit, all the classics.

'Wow, Jill, you look *so* much better now,' he said, smiling widely at her.

'Er… thanks. I think,' she said, looking at me with a raised eyebrow.

'*So* much better than before! You really are looking very good these days!'

Afterwards she said to me, 'I think your dad thought he was giving me a compliment.'

I've inherited his propensity to talk to strangers, I'm happy to strike up conversation with anyone, and in this way I like being like him. It comes easily to me, I seem to be able to forge connections quickly and lightly that hold strong over time, but still these invitations surprised me, especially at this time of disconnection, of infection. To be invited now felt especially generous.

The way I met Giorgia was by sitting on a rock at Cala Rotonda in a towel in November. There's a thin arch formation here that rises from the sea and frames the bay. I'd been swimming laps and was sitting in the sun to warm up. Giorgia was about twenty-five years old, and had something of the old Italian movie stars about her: curly black hair, a trench coat, dark sunglasses, and an elegant way of holding her body against the light.

'*Buongiorno*,' she said.

'*Buongiorno*,' I replied, and when she heard my accent she switched into perfect English.

'You've been swimming? But it's so cold!' She told me she swims once a year, at the very height of summer, and even then only under duress. 'There are snakes in this water, many, many snakes,' she said.

I think she meant eels, but it was a bit discomforting. Then she pointed at her mother and father, a little way up the beach.

'Now we will go to eat something, would you like to join us?'

Later, Giorgia told me that she would never normally strike up conversation with a stranger but she saw that I was alone and 'forgotten by god' so she thought she'd invite me to be with her family. She gave me the address, got into an ancient Fiat Panda, the kind of car that all the islanders drove, and inched it over the potholes in the track back from the beach. I followed on my bike. Later I learned that the arc-shaped formation of the rocks here is called the Arco di Ulisse (the Italian form of Odysseus, from the Latin Ulixes). Perhaps he brought her to me. At this point I was willing to believe more than ever in coincidence, in serendipity.

A real Sicilian family, a feast. Everything I had ever hoped from home-made Italian cooking. Giorgia, Ignazio her father, Stella her mother, and Susana and Angelo, her aunt and uncle, were all there, all talking loudly over each other in the best Italian style. They lived across the water in Trapani but kept a house on the island and Giorgia had spent every childhood summer here, knew every inch of it. We ate in the garden surrounded by cactus plants. I was consulted about this year's oil by Ignazio, she translated.

'He wants to know, how does it taste?'

He looked at me expectantly, brows furrowed, as I dipped my bread in the greenest, thickest olive oil I'd ever seen.

'*Buono!*' I said, taking my time over the syllables. It was newly pressed, which was why it was such an extraordinary vibrant green, and it tasted slightly spicy, unlike any oil I'd tried before. There was lasagne and *linguine al nero di seppia* (pasta with cuttlefish ink), inky black with a salty, umami taste, and little fried fish eaten whole and cakes from the Pasticceria which shone like jewels. The meal lasted over four hours. I loved being with a family again, feeling part of everything, even if Giorgia had to simultaneously translate me to them. Afterwards we drank absurdly tiny coffees and ate *frutta martorana,* made from almonds, sugar and water, shaped and painted to look like fruit and vegetables. They tasted like a lighter version of marzipan.

'This is a very typical Sicilian dessert,' Giorgia said, 'we make them for the *Giorno dei Morti*, the Day of the Dead, everyone will be taking flowers to the graveyard.' She explained that these sweets are given to children by the *morti*, their dead relatives, to help forge connections across the generations even when people are no longer alive. A far lovelier version of Halloween.

After lunch we went over to the cemetery by the sea, every grave had bunches of big yellow flowers. No one had been forgotten. There was something gorgeous about this commemoration – I'd never seen a cemetery bursting with flowers like this before. It felt oddly cheering, the dead were remembered, missed, loved.

'Would you like to see some open-air caves?' Giorgia asked mysteriously. As we drove over to the north-eastern tip of the island she told me the ancient Romans came here to quarry the strong white *tufo* stone (calcarenite arenaria) for their fancy Sicilian houses on the mainland. Quarrying here really exploded from the seventeenth century and this legacy shaped the landscape into something other-worldly. There were sudden sheer drops either side of the road down into quarry pits up to thirty metres deep. We wandered around the strange free-standing vertical stacks of rocks far below street level in the *labirinto*. They made me feel slightly vertiginous as we went deeper and the labyrinth unfolded. Giorgia, who knew all this from her summer job as a tour guide, said some of the most extensive quarries had been turned into extraordinary sunken gardens for rich people with second houses on the island. She pointed out the literal marks of the past at the sea cliffs at Cala Rossa and Bue Marino beaches, where steps had been carved into the stone to form a ladder, and the hand-chiselled grid lines were distinctive from later machine-made ones. We climbed to the top of one of the stacks and Giorgia's father took a photograph of us, high up, outlined against the blue sky.

Where the water has reclaimed the scars of the quarries, lagoons and shallow turquoise swimming pools have formed. On the way back we stopped at Scalo Cavallo, a lagoon named for a rock that looks like a horse and the prettiest name of all to say out loud. There were stone steps and a wobbly rail down into witch-green waters which shelved down deeper and darker, turning emerald and then black-green, until it felt like I was swimming over the abyss.

When we returned, Giorgia's father made us all drink shots of Mirto, his moonshine made from bitter myrtle leaves. I looked at them, father and daughter laughing together, and raised a toast. The liquid burned down my throat.

Days without edges elided, time slipped its claws as November ran on. My loneliness changed, persistent but no longer combined with emptiness. A fuller kind of loneliness replaced it, filled by ritual – swims and cycles, regulated by the dawns and dusks and sunsets by which I flowed my days. I had instinctively moved back to caveman-ish circadian rhythms, with the world in hibernation, I became enmeshed, attuned to weather systems. As the month deepened into winter my eyes sharpened, locking on to tiny gradients of changes. The changing weight of the moon, a shifting of the wind as the day spun open, a new kind of pastry in the bakery window to mark a particular holy day. The hay in the fields, first mown and then baled, the changing colours of the scrubby bushes around the coves. Little increments of change that ordinarily I would have sped past, rushed over. I started to pay more attention to everything, the liquid neon dart of a green lizard I interrupted sunbathing. The way the birds jinked and surfed. I remained alone but somehow the world expanded, had grown larger around me on this 'island full of wonders', far larger than it was in my big, mutable city. It had become my sea-kingdom, an Ithaca, a new home. I had grown quite unlike myself, more like myself, made from light and salt and sea.

Enchantment is not always passive, you don't have to bite into the apple and choke and fall into a coma. It can be something chosen, a placing of attention. In *The Odyssey* there's plenty of different enchantments. The witch Circe turns the crew into swine, drug addict Lotus Eaters get them high on plant medicine, Helen of Troy spikes the wine with a drug that takes away the bitter feeling of grief, gods turn into birds, and Athena disguises or enhances Odysseus's appearance at various points to make him more handsome, older or younger. Sirens sing sexy death-metal songs to men who can't resist their call (oh, how the patriarchy fears women) and I think how often I've been enchanted by regret, pulled back to the past. But there are positive enchantments in the story too. Gods are believed in, prayed to, libations are offered to them, sacrifices are made to their glory. To be charmed, enthralled, spellbound requires belief in the magic, clapping for Tinker Bell.

The word 'enchantment' is a singing word, derived from the word for song. Built into its etymology is 'fascination', 'being charmed', literally under a charm, it sings us back to ourselves. It's the way that donkeys looked at me with the liquid eyes of poets before crying melancholically in their rust voices, the movement of black sea butterflies that skimmed the waves, surfing out far from shore, accompanying my swims. The strange sweet-smelling purple flowers by the shore that looked slightly witchy. I asked and was told they were mandragora, the ancient sedative that I'd craved in lockdown, the drug Cleopatra demanded when Antony left her and she wanted to 'sleep out this great gap of time'. Seeing these purple flowers was proof, in case I needed it, that everything circles. *Incantesimo* is the Italian for spell and if you say it aloud you can hear how it contains the sound of a wand striking, with its emphasised middle syllables.

I built a map of the island, knew it instinctively now, how fast the unknown becomes familiar with repetition, becomes loved. I felt a settling, something slowing down and uncurling. Part of home is being known, but it's also knowing a place.

As I re-established rhythm, contours, I felt less dissolved. Or rather, that something was clarifying, joining together again. Rebuilding. I was getting physically stronger, my body weaving new muscles, my spine felt more fluid, it was no longer like I was held up by wires pushed through my veins like in lockdown. Every day felt Sundayish. I worked but did more than that. In London I'd crouched low over my laptop all day, leaving and returning home in the dark like an animal, eyes aching from epileptic bicycle lights, and neon high-vis, and car beams that lanced the night, obscuring the stars, tired from the aggression of drivers, from the cold damp, my thin waterproof jacket scant protection against the rain, the weight of the city, the fear of being crushed by a left-turning lorry. Here my work was more integrated. The small size of the island meant I could eat lunch by the water almost every day, my new routine meant I started each morning by plunging into the sea.

In the cold I was all function, no longer form, I could slip away from my mind and go into my body, held in the sea salt. My focus narrowed to forcing my breath to slow, breathing from my gills. Blue after blue, salt on salt. I watched the diamond-shaped light on water rippling squamous cells onto my skin, stayed as close to the sea's edges as I could, listened for it while I slept.

I sat in the shade at Cala Pierrca, with my journal, a book and a water bottle. The ocean was flaunting its jewels, aquamarine and sapphire and blue topaz and crystalline diamonds sparkled. The sun was soft and sweet, pressing against the fortitude of the rocks, warming the stones. It wasn't a room I wanted but a cove of one's own. I watched the sea lick salt from the rocks, sand-coloured minnows swimming in the shallows. The sea shaded itself, changed its mind, remixed its blues, the deeps, the shallows. Weaving and unweaving, just like Penelope. Aeolus made the brown seaweed strands dance in the wind. I stretched out, shifting the pebbles under my body, and napped in my jumper in the warm winter sun. Romance for one. 'Lift up your hearts,' intoned the memory priest of my childhood sternly, and the congregation responded as one: 'We lift them up to the Lord.' There's something in that. Lift up your heart. My swollen, salt-sated heart.

'He's terribly proud of you, he loves telling his friends about your island,' said my mother, who more and more acted as my father's unofficial spokesperson. 'He's not really very well at the moment,' she said quietly as if less volume would make it less true. She desperately wanted the new treatment to work. Another spell, another enchantment, but a violent kind of magic this time. Faith and medicine are linked – the placebo effect shows how powerful belief can be. Sometimes with cancer, to get better, you have to get sicker first, that's how the medicine works.

I dreamt of my father that night, dwarfish and shrunken in a white jumper. 'He wants to pay the bill,' says my dream mother, 'let him pay.' The dream was layers of sad, his and mine. My father shrinking and holding a politician's hand, like he was a child, trying to make his point, I was trying to protect him from the derision of the politician. He had confronted David Cameron once back when he was prime minister about health reforms that he thought negatively affected GPs. He'd booked an appointment, prepared his points scrupulously, rehearsed, he wanted to make a difference. Nothing changed.

When I woke up, I called him and floated the idea of making a podcast but it was too late, too complicated – we'd need specialist equipment, he said. I should have made my request smaller, just recorded our phone calls. Laura is/was my daughter. Is/Was. Is and Was. For now. Topics I wanted to interview him about: what will you miss, regret, remember? What is death, religion, love? What stories do you have of all the patients you treated? Anger. Diplomacy. Brain surgery. What would you have done differently? What should I do, what should I do, what should I do?

All day the weather had been headachy and oppressive. Change was coming. I cycled over to Cala Rossa in the east. It was a striking place full of odd rock formations left over from all that quarrying and a long curve out to a point. The weather broke just after I arrived, a huge thunderstorm turned the sea milky and the sky a strange dark pink colour. Despite the danger, I slipped into the water and swam across the bay watching lightning crackle the sky, Zeus and Poseidon nearby. Afterwards I felt filled with a sort of metallic energy as I cycled back soaking wet and invincible.

The Odyssey is full of storms and thunderbolts, they create tension, drive the plot, illustrate the fury of the gods, the power of fate and nature, kill the crew, and test Odysseus as a character. I liked storms but I was tired of being tested. I wanted everything to go back to normal.

The morning after the storm, in the new freshness, as I climbed up to the castle, the mountain pulsed green against the sharpness of the early light. The fort at the top was originally built by Saracen invaders who captured the island in the Middle Ages and used it as a launch pad for their conquest of Sicily. It was subsequently built and rebuilt by successions of various conquerors but now it was a spooky place full of weird abandoned satellite equipment left to rust under the open sky. Castles are often better appreciated from a distance. I liked to watch it from my balcony in the abandoned hotel – it was illuminated at night and often looked like there were special effects playing across it, as the interplay of the clouds and the moon could make it seem misty and gothic and foreboding or fairy-tale princessy. I left my curtains open for Dawn to wake me so the castle was the first thing I saw when I woke up. I still reflexively checked my phone for a text which never came and the urge to call my ex-boyfriend was something I had to bite down each morning. I looked up at the castle on the hill, and thought of fairy stories and the lies we tell little girls.

Even after the storm something remained unresolved in the air. Giorgia said, with the elegant half-shrug Italians are born with, that it was possible that Sicily would be designated a *zona arancia* (orange zone), which involved additional restrictions and the threat of more to come. My stomach clenched. A familiar lurch of panic. Jungle living, drinking at the waterhole, ears pricked, legs tense. Should I throw in the towel and go home, or stay? I didn't want to be locked down again in either place. London's infection rate was ticking up dramatically and I decided fast this time. The idea of going back to a known loneliness was worse than dealing with the unknown, which at least contained within it possibility. On the island the restaurants were ordered to close – Bar Cono became takeaway only.

I called my father. Being sad about anything to a terminal cancer patient feels petty, rude, disrespectful. Cancer is selfish, steals all the space, inculcates guilt. Anticipatory grief is wearing, exhausting for everyone. But he liked turning advisor and diplomat, he was far more cool-headed than I am so I brought my petty problems to him anyway, and laid them down, a dead mouse offering.

'It's like I've been living in the present tense,' I said, 'fully in the moment and now I'm having to think about the future again and I'm scared.'

'Your mother thinks you should come home.'

'This feels like home,' I said. London felt distant. I preferred who I was here, on an island, in translation.

'Well, Pietro, you can always find another island,' he said, 'I'd stay out of the UK as long as you can. I rather like the idea of you swimming with jellyfish.'

The island didn't know it had been designated *arancia*, continued on being radiant, the birds still wheeled in the air, bats looped in the lanes at dusk, at sunset there were still graffiti clouds, neon orange, hot pink, highlighter yellow. I called the Trailfinders travel agent and he asked breezily where I wanted to go. An upbeat, professional voice. As if there was a choice instead of a set of constraints, as if the flight paths were not all broken. Going home would be a surrender to the darkness and to winter, to shadow and stillness. When I pictured my flat, the walls kept moving in, crushing me, I could feel panic rising. All the things I'd found that balanced me, made me normal again here, the birds and the swimming, none of them were in London. Without water and the sunlight I thought I might go grey again. I had touched something closely in that first lockdown, something that sat in the greyness, something that could engulf me and I knew I needed to stay as far away from that as I could.

I started to fill in the paperwork to leave Italy. Where next? I'd followed *The Odyssey* to the kingdom of the winds, to Ithaca, and to this 'island full of wonders', perhaps the myth could guide me again. My magnets were scrambled, I didn't have another kind of compass.

What shall—
what should I do? And the sea says
In its lovely voice:
Excuse me, I have work to do.

The enchantment was broken, the dream ended. I longed for the island before I even left.

Chapter Seven

From the Goddess to the Storm

Calypso on Korčula, Croatia

There sat Calypso with her braided curls.
Beside the hearth a mighty fire was burning.
The scent of citrus and of brittle pine
suffused the island. Inside, she was singing
and weaving with a shuttle made of gold.
Her voice was beautiful. Around the cave
a luscious forest flourished: alder, poplar
and scented cypress. It was full of wings.
Birds nested there but hunted out at sea

After the ethereal beauties of my sunlit Italian islands, Split, the busy main port halfway up Croatia, was a shock, cold, dark and crowded. I'd lost an hour of sunlight and several degrees of warmth by coming here. I didn't like being back in a city again, the press of people, the traffic noise, I stocked up on new pens and it wasn't a joy like it had been in Lipari – just another anonymous transaction in a strip-lit shop.

Cities were all I wanted when I was younger, growing up in an isolated rural village where nothing ever happened and serenity felt like a trap. I craved scale and intensity, the non-stop energy of London, the electrical lights of New York, to take me away from myself, places to get lost and find the unknown, but now I wanted to be away from it all in the sleepy quiet of a cove. Give me a beach house by the sea, and a language I don't speak, and the sun blazing down in winter. The cold here was sharp. I bought the warmest coat I could find in town.

The Dalmatian coast conjures a whirl of polka dots every time for me. The last time I visited was under very different circumstances, in the old order, with an old boyfriend in tow. We went to Hvar because I couldn't think where else to go. It became a sort of a Russian dolls holiday because, many years before, in my twirling optimistic twenties, I'd visited the same island for the first time with my first blazing love. I felt odd and dislocated being back, between the ghost of the first and the shadow of the second. Back again now in Split, I was sharply nostalgic for my younger self. I was blonde then, and assured, travelling with a backpack and no money, wildly in love with the boyfriend, who kept us both half-starved all trip, forbidding lunch in his attempt to lose weight. We'd caught the boat from Venice to Croatia, sleeping out on the deck all night to save the cost of booking a cabin. There's a photograph I still have that he took of me, sitting at a restaurant table in a pink t-shirt, my face covered in new freckles. I'm smiling like nothing would ever change. We were always within touching distance on that trip, I was tucked under his arm as he showed me the world and the ease with which the rich occupy it. I wanted to travel backwards to how it used to be, when I was twenty-one and nothing was on the internet and we were met at bus stations by old ladies with signs for rooms, no pictures or online reviews, you just followed one of them and hoped for the best and it all worked out, everything bright with possibility. This time felt very different. I was alone, it was winter and dark. I wanted to be that girl again.

In the 1970s Aristid Vučetić, who lived in Dubrovnik, suggested that the primary location for Odysseus's journey was the Adriatic, rather than the Aegean, and argued that the Croatian island of Mljet was Calypso's island for a number of reasons, including the fact that it has a cave which fits the description in the story. According to the book *Demystifying the Odyssey*, when Vučetić published his ideas in a series of newspaper articles, furious Italian scholars immediately sought to discredit this 'attempt to displace Odysseus's travels'. His theory may not have been robust enough to convince Italian experts, but it was good enough for me.

There was no direct ferry to Mljet so I bought a ticket to Korčula, the nearest island, planning to spend a few days there before finding a way to hop over. The boat moved slowly through the water taking me south, in the direction of Montenegro.

Korčula is long and thin – about thirty-two kilometres in length and eight kilometres across, and famous for its fairy-tale town which is smaller and prettier than Dubrovnik. I rented a small, warm apartment from Adrijana, above an artist's studio deep in the middle of the walled city. Designed by clever Venetian colonialists, the narrow streets are set out in a fish-bone pattern, each one curved and angled off a central spine to protect residents from the howls of the *Bura* (bora), a heavy, deeply unpleasant katabatic type of wind that blows from the north-east, and to allow the lovely north-western *Maestral* (mistral) wind to bring fresh air during the hot summer. The power of winds on islands was reinforced to me once again as I wandered through the streets – supposedly, a law was passed here back in mediaeval times granting immunity from prosecution on days that the south-easterly *Jugo* wind was strong, because it was said to send people out of their minds, and naturally they couldn't possibly be held responsible for criminal behaviour when the wind was high. I could see the Venetian influence on the town with its elegant white buildings. The whole place looked like it had been carved out of marble but there were very few tourists and it felt eerily empty, a toy town with no dolls.

I met Joey The Innocent walking through the streets. He was an American student in his early twenties, tall and thin, a handsome nerd with wire-framed glasses, an innocently wide-eyed enthusiastic take on life, and a sparse goatee that he occasionally stroked, as if trying to encourage it to grow. His lectures had moved online and he'd travelled to Croatia because it was still open to tourists, infection rates were low, living costs were cheap, and he wanted to see the islands. I explained my plan to visit Mljet and Joey looked at me with concern. 'It was terrible there,' he said, 'everything was closed and it was foggy and spooky. Like being in a horror film, the part when you're just about to be killed.' As he talked I pictured a forbidding island, cold and damp, grey and sinister.

In the story, Calypso's island sounds more like an expensive scented candle:

The scent of citrus and of brittle pine
Suffused the island...

Divine Calypso lives in a cave in the middle of her perfumed forest. Odysseus washes up on her shores after surviving the shipwreck that Zeus caused when his men ate the sun god's cattle. The goddess seduces him, I think by deploying the fail-safe and deeply erotic art of loom-weaving, and by singing a bit, it's not totally clear, although of course her promise of immortality probably helps. Anyway, Odysseus, for his part, pleasures Calypso so expertly that she's never sated and becomes determined to keep him around. Basically, she imprisons him as her sex slave for seven years. Presumably, epic sex with a beautiful goddess wasn't the worst deal for him either. Although when we first meet Odysseus in the story, he is crying on the beach, longing for home and missing his wife, who he's cheating on.

The story starts in the middle, with Athena persuading Zeus that Odysseus must be allowed to go home. 'Swift-flashing' Hermes (the on-demand courier god) is dispatched to Calypso with a message telling her to get her claws out of Odysseus and release him. The goddess does not think it's a vibe that she's being asked to give up her lover, and launches into an impassioned feminist speech:

Calypso shuddered and let fly at him
you cruel, jealous gods! You bear a grudge
whenever any goddess takes a man
to sleep with as a lover in her bed

It's a powerful takedown and she backs up every point she makes: gorgeous, rosy Dawn took the mortal Orion for a lover, only for

Artemis to slaughter him. Demeter, goddess of the harvest, made sweet love with Iasion in the fields, until Zeus firebombed him to death. It's a man's world even when you're a goddess – same old double standards. Calypso must submit to Zeus's will, she doesn't have a choice because, like it always is, power is concentrated in the hands of men.

Accordingly, she gives Odysseus detailed, Ikea-like instructions on how to build a raft and supplies him with food and drink, clothes and a soft wind to blow him safely home. Odysseus is emotional and histrionic about the idea of sailing away on a flimsy little raft, is paranoid it's a trick, makes her reassure him. Calypso for her part tries to understand why he wants to return to Penelope, a mere mortal, when she's a smoking-hot goddess queen. It's a good question:

I know my body is better than hers is. I am taller too.
Mortals can never rival the immortals in beauty

She ends up reasoning that it must be because Odysseus is masochistically drawn to suffering. Never missing a beat, he agrees, and starts to flatter her. Now he knows he's about to head home to his wife, all the tears have dried up and he's up for one last epic session.

they went inside the hollow cave
and took the pleasure of their love, held close together

Emily Wilson argues that Calypso's speech is memorable because of its emotional openness but points out that she 'does herself a disservice by only emphasising her superior good looks. She also has a superior mind'. Emily believes the goddess 'appreciates and understands [his] capacity for deceit and scheming because she has similar qualities herself' and therefore is particularly well matched with him.

For me, it was annoyingly resonant, an insecure goddess worrying about her appearance, getting twisted up by an undeserving man, and doubting herself.

I called my father but he sounded distracted.

'What are you doing?'

'I'm watching TV.'

'Really? I thought you were writing my wedding speech.'

'Don't be annoying,' he said sharply, 'I'm struggling a bit today, Pietro.' This was his code for a horrific day full of pain and nausea and slamming tiredness. Cancer treatments have nefarious side effects, irritation was the least of it.

'Okay – let's talk later,' I said.

I called my brother. He said not to worry too much, reassured me it was all normal. In two weeks he'd get a break to allow his body to recover.

I put the phone down, thinking about pain and all the different forms it can take.

The Adriatic waters were green and deliciously icy but swimming in Korčula was significantly more bracing than swimming in Italy. The water was palpably colder and the outside temperature had dropped as well, so it was freezing when I got in, and cold when I got out. But by now I was dependent on the shock, the surge of adrenaline, the blast of endorphins. I set out to find all the best swimming spots on the island during my first weekend. At Pupnatska Luca, on the south coast, the beach looked like a postcard-promise: a half-circle of electric-blue water framed by bright green pine forests, with high mountains rising up both sides of the bay.

I'd hired an electric bicycle to get here. Normally, I'd consider that cheating but the road was too steep for a regular bike to handle, and even the sophisticated machine struggled with some of the ascents. The final winding descent had me gripping the handlebars too tightly as I whizzed down the twisty mountain road, taking the corners too fast. The beach was pebbly and the water was breathtakingly cold by this point in deep midwinter as I slowly walked in. I hesitated when it reached up my thighs and forced myself to submerge, attempting to control my staccato breath as needles burst all over my skin. I tried, as always, to observe the way the cold moved over my body, paying attention to how it radiated across me, flaring down into my wrists as my breath choked in my throat.

I'm a strong swimmer, built for it, something that my father delighted in saying, supposing it to be a huge compliment, until my mother pointed out he was giving me a complex. 'Broad shoulders compared to your waist,' he corrected, missing the point. 'I just mean you're athletic,' he said sadly, 'your shoulders are nicely muscular,' giving my mother an eye-roll that meant the delicacy of teenage girls was off the scale. I've never worn strapless dresses but I've always loved to swim. After a few minutes I started to feel the high, thrill overtaking discomfort, and it became easy to slip among the waves as I swam laps across the bay. I shook almost uncontrollably from the cold when I got out, my body flushed red all over, my white frozen fingers not working properly, fumbling with my clothes.

At Samograd bay on the opposite shore, near the village of Račišće, fifteen kilometres west of town, something went wrong with the electric bike and I ended up covered in oil, calling the bike shop and waiting for Antonija to drive over with a fresh battery, as the bike was too heavy to pedal uphill with no power, but the swim, when I got there, was worth the drama.

The beach was shingle and the sea moved over the pebbles making a sound like a gambler rolling dice at a poker table. I swam into the reflection of the green pine trees which made the water seem even greener than normal. The Greeks called this island 'Black Korčula' on account of the density of its pine trees, and the island is still mostly covered in forests today.

When I swim it feels like I've found a way to reoccupy my body, forcing it into freezing water seems to soothe the usually inescapable percolating anxieties that it holds, and days when I don't swim, for whatever reason, feel flat and contourless. I had managed to extend my freelance work again but with the days getting shorter balancing meetings with the craven demands of my cold water addicted body was becoming increasingly tricky, it was too cold for evening swims after dark, and too dark for morning swims before work.

My usual weekday spot became Mandrač 'beach', beneath the monastery just outside the town. If I walked fast I could usually fit in a quick dip around lunchtime. It's not really a beach, it's a small port on the western side, where locals keep their wooden boats. The name comes from *mandraccio*, little harbour, in Italian, the collision of language thanks to Venetian colonisation. The water was always placid here, more like a lake than the sea. I turned onto my back and floated, looking at the fairy-tale town, the skyline dominated by the bell tower of the church, red-roofed houses, extravagant palm trees and the huge fortified city walls hugging it all together. The view was beautiful but I missed the rough Italian waves, being bounced and tossed around. There was no sense of danger here swimming among the bobbing boats.

One day, rushing for a dip between meetings, I saw a blonde woman cutting through the water in style. A black cormorant and I watched her from the shore and when I joined her in the sea, screaming out from the cold, she laughed and suggested I slip in more quietly, conserving my energy. Afterwards she invited me to share a flask of hot tea to warm up.

Toned and slight, Lea was in her forties but looked younger. She was a practitioner of yoga and a believer in writing letters to the moon. The letters had to be written on green paper and slipped under your pillow a few nights before the full moon. She also believed in wearing beautiful lingerie, the power of whole foods to restore the body, the health benefits of cold water swimming, and never losing yourself in a relationship. There was something elevated, something other-worldly about her. When she told me her father was originally from Mljet it clicked into place. Lea could have been an incarnation of Calypso, or at least one of her descendants.

She quickly became my nutritionist and doctor. Trained as a phyto-aromatherapist, Lea knew about how to mix oil elixirs and which plant extracts nourish and uplift. She prescribed a strict diet of coming to her house to eat bright orange pumpkin soup with toasted seeds that cracked when I bit into them, and bitter tangerine brownies, made from the winter fruit still clinging to her tree. She made me buy a bewildering set of supplements, sternly telling me they were all critical when I wondered how I'd fit them into my suitcase when I left. I followed her instructions to cleanse my stressed-out liver with black radish and artichoke, took foul-tasting garlic ointment to ward off winter colds, added drops of vitamin D to my water and swallowed awkwardly large spirulina tablets every day.

Lea blended bespoke aromatherapy oils precisely mixed to address all my various pathological needs, which she identified with alarming accuracy, red mandarin for lifting the spirits, sage for femininity, ylang-ylang for 'falling in love with yourself'. They smelt of citrus and the woods, like Calypso's forest. She also gave me something made from marine magnesium that she promised would heal my fractured sleep. This had been an unexpected casualty to the pandemic and to new fears that come in the shadows, with death and endings on their breath. I used to sleep beautifully, rocking down into the depths whenever I wanted, but now I woke fretting in strange beds looking up at unfamiliar ceilings in the middle of the night, every night, and could not sleep again.

Sugar was banned but Lea made me a dense chocolate cake without it, served with a type of golden-yellow jam she'd made back in the summer. We ate the heavy, tangy cake after swimming together at the large open-air pool on the outskirts of town. Lea told me that in the seventies, against all odds, Korčula's team romped home to a surprise victory in the European water polo cup – the smallest town ever to hold this title. The outside pool had been made for the islanders to practise in but in winter it was empty.

I followed Lea's instructions, swallowed all the pills, applied the oil, tried to think beautiful thoughts. Her prescription gave me my first unbroken night's sleep in months. On Korčula I was reconnecting with a 'yes' that in London was more often a 'no', when

I was speeding around the city on my bicycle, oscillating between work and yoga classes (where ironically I never slowed down at all), between seeing friends and attending work dinners, between going to comedy nights, going on dates, going to ice-skating lessons, and getting on planes. When all that stopped, something deep in me had become fossilised, begun to turn brittle, but under Lea's watchful eye I started to gather my powers again, powers which had scattered so far from me in the pandemic that I barely remembered how to use them. Lea reminded me of what I used to know, gave me her scarf against the chill wind, and swam alongside me. Perhaps she was a mix of Circe and Calypso after all – part witch, part goddess. Either way, with Lea I started to trust myself again, connect back to my intuition. And I realised after a few days of this new regime that I hadn't checked my phone all day, that I was no longer half-hoping my ex-boyfriend would suddenly show up on the island with arms full of flowers and eyes full of sorrow. That I actually hadn't thought about him at all.

To reach Mljet, Lea said I'd need to take a convoluted route which involved returning to the mainland and catching the car ferry back again, but warned me it was a bad time of the year to visit, and she thought the weather was about to turn worse. Clairvoyance seemed to be another of her magical skills because the next day, there was a storm, the sea became too dangerous to cross, and ferries were indefinitely suspended. 'This happens in winter,' I was told with a shrug by people at the port when I asked when I could leave. The week stretched out and still there were no boats. Odysseus and I had swapped places: I was trapped on the wrong island while he faced the storm at sea.

When Odysseus floats off on his raft, his powerful enemy Poseidon spies him. In a furious rage he whips the sea into a tempest. Seasick and lurching, Odysseus moans and complains, falls off, manages to clamber back on, and needs to be rescued by a woman, yet again. This time it's the white goddess, Ino, who takes the form of a gull. She instructs him to strip naked, tie her scarf to him as protection, abandon the splintering raft and jump overboard. Stubborn, faithless Odysseus doesn't follow her instructions, but eventually his raft gets so smashed up he has no choice. Ino's plan works exactly as she said it would, and then yet another woman steps in to help him. This time it's Athena, who protects Odysseus, one of her all-time favourites. She soothes the winds, calming the sea so that he can swim to the shore of yet another island, cheating death once again.

I don't much dream of being rescued by gulls and goddesses, but not being able to leave because of the storm showed me the flip side of islands – the isolation that's intrinsic to them – they can be places to escape to until you can't leave, and then they become something else entirely. I don't like feeling trapped, having no way out. I always have an exit plan, need to feel there's a door or window open at all times. I think it came from being raised in the deep countryside, with no public transport I was stuck, there was no escape. I just had to wait until I got old enough to drive, until I got old enough to leave.

I headed over to Frano's restaurant, Konoba Komin, to soothe myself by his fire.

Frano looked like a pirate captain, his long silver hair tied back with a bandana, and he dressed entirely in black. The food he cooked was simple and delicious, barbequed over the open fire, but his restaurant was usually empty. Most days it was just the two of us, shooting the breeze over black cuttlefish risotto or bakalar soup made from white fish and potatoes, but today the door opened and in from the storm blew a red-headed American woman, shaking out her curls. Behind her, a svelte, good-looking man in an elegant scarf fought against the wind to lower his umbrella. They took the table nearest the fire and she invited me to join them for a glass of Pošip, the local wine. In an example of perfect normative determinism, she told me her name was Mona and she was a sex therapist.

I didn't plan to be doing a moon ritual with a sex therapist and yet here I was, on the rocks, late at night lighting candles. When I asked Mona what her job was like she said it was mainly listening to people, not being judgemental, reassuring them. Then she told me in a loud stage whisper that Georges, her French boyfriend, 'is quite conservative in bed' and he looked up at that, aghast, and quickly tried to hide it as she laughed.

Mona lived in Florida and commuted by paddleboard down the river to her office, Georges wore an actual cravat and lived in Paris. Neither of them wanted to move. The compromise, somehow, was buying a summer house in Korčula. And here the three of us were, at midnight on the rocks underneath the city walls.

It had stopped raining but it was still stormy, the sea was noisy and bright, crashing against the black rocks, fast-moving clouds traced across the yellow of the moon, catching its glow. Following instructions from the internet, not being conversant in moon rituals, Mona tied three candles together with blue string. I was instructed to ceremonially cut the string around the first candle which represented the past. We each wrote down what we needed to leave behind and burned it in the flame. I scribbled the name of the boy who inspired my reading of *The Odyssey*. He was the catalyst for this journey, his actions set me in motion, and after all, isn't adventure the next best thing to love? Tiny leaping sparks flew into the black night as the paper flamed.

The second candle was what we were thankful for. I wrote a long list of names of people who'd been kind to me on this journey. Again the paper burned orange against the dark.

The third candle was the future. I wrote things my younger self would have scoffed at, stupidly conventional things. Then we sat cross-legged on the damp rocks and tried to feel moonlight and starlight inside us. I ended up just listening to the sea clanging against the city walls, thinking how much I liked Mona's openness, her vibrancy. When I opened my eyes, Georges, biting down on a smile, was picking up bits of string and burned out candles. I looked up at the round moon, at the moonlight silvering the dark, restless sea, hoping at least some of it would come true.

The next day, in the second-hand bookshop in town I randomly opened a poetry book at this poem. It sounds contrived, like something convenient in a movie, but it really happened. Maybe the ritual was working. Perhaps I was being guided, after all.

Is it

possible
to be returning
all your life
to a Penelope
you've
never met

Adrijana, my landlord, invited me to her home for a traditional Serbian lunch. Her aunt and uncle were there, normally they spent the winter in Belgrade but like me they felt it was far safer to stay out of big cities. Adrijana's house was bright with paintings, the lair of an artist. We ate soup and a type of sauerkraut dish served with roast pork but the best bit of the meal was *tufahije* – baked green apples stuffed with a delightful mixture of chocolate and hazelnuts. Adrijana's uncle had made them. He set my plate in front of me ceremonially, violently shook the canister as if it had deeply offended him, and proceeded to cover my apple with an impossibly vertical amount of whipped cream. Without language between us, we smiled at each other like children. The apple tasted like a benediction, like something Odysseus and his men would have given their right arms for as they starved on various islands. In the story they are often hungry, and of course this hunger is not just physical but symbolic of their longing for home.

After lunch, Adrijana took me to Crkva Svetog Antuna (the Church of St Anthony). Perched at the top of a hundred stairs, each step flanked by tall cypress trees, the walk up felt grand and ceremonial, but the church itself was simple with a little bell tower and a fourteenth-century carving of the saint dominated by a huge love heart. We sat on a bench outside looking out at the sea whipped by the high winds. I asked how Adrijana had come to this island from Serbia and she told me it was a love story. She fell in love with a man from Korčula, and had a child. Although their marriage didn't end up lasting, her love of the island held strong. Tall and athletic, she reminded me somehow of a panther. It occurred to me as I listened to her that Adrijana was perhaps another version of charismatic, seductive Calypso. There was a quality of self-containment to her, a powerful sort of assurance I admired, lacking it myself.

As she talked I also saw her determination, raising her son as a single mother, adopting this island, forging her home here, building her business, first the art shop, then the rental flat, and soon a new hotel from the ruins of a Venetian palace. There was something charged about her, something electrical. She was almost fifty and filled with energy, as she moved lightly across her adopted land. When she dropped me back at my apartment she worried about the chill and insisted on lending me a warm mohair jumper. Wearing it made me feel close to her, I hoped some of her way of being might be transmitted to me.

When I leave this island, I'll give her mohair jumper back, against her protestations, something I'll later come to regret. I'll wish I'd kept it, kept a piece of her near me. Clothes and jewellery carry something of their owners, I think, deep inside the strands of the fabric, invisible, like DNA.

Sartorially, my father dressed with one single purpose in mind: to foil the evil intentions of would-be pickpockets. This began with a pair of waterproof trousers with zip-up pockets whose thief-proof benefits he'd extol enthusiastically. These mortified me as a teenager and promises were extorted that he'd never step out of the car when picking me up. A bumbag was a fixture for many years and while this was pretty good at deterring potential bandits, he reached weapons-grade security level with the purchase of a wallet on a chain. This majestic device never let him down as he roamed through the dangerous Cotswolds.

When I'd last seen him he'd slipped one of his cashmere jumpers into my bag. I found it when I got back to London and was touched, he wasn't usually one for presents. When I was home I'd borrow his socks and jumpers but it was always unauthorised. I folded it carefully in a bag to protect it from moths and put it into a drawer. I wished I'd brought his jumper with me. I could have used it in this Croatian cold.

He believed in rituals too. Every time they went for a hospital appointment, he and my mother would dress as smartly as possible. I think he believed in a way that making an effort might increase the chances of good news.

———————

The weather got worse, the winds continued to be too high for the boats. I began to accept I wouldn't reach Mljet, would never make it to Calypso's island after all. That's the thing with odysseys, you don't really get to choose where you go, it's down to fate and the gods.

Restrictions tightened, Frano was forced to close his restaurant, our evening conversations by the fire were removed, and life started to lose its colour. All the cafes became takeaway only and without cafes and restaurants there was nowhere to go. The old loneliness cut tighter, bit harder. I determined to travel up to Zagreb and catch a flight out of the country as soon as the ferries started to run again. It felt like winter was drawing in, that things were getting worse.

———————

I swam in the rain and started thinking again about the idea of home, and my migration paths to and from it. Perhaps every time home gets redefined, our losses get greater. I'd been reading about homing pigeons, how they carried messages from the troops to command in the First World War. Pigeons were way more reliable than radio equipment back then. The courageous birds flew high above the battlefields, swerving bullets, even as snipers trained their guns on them, ordered to disrupt enemy communications by trying to shoot them down. The interesting thing is that you can train a homing pigeon to fly back to different places. The birds can be taught that home is a moveable concept, that it's not always fixed. Even pigeons can understand that things rarely stay the same for long. The bird learns and she adapts after just a few training flights, using her mysterious magnetic senses to lock on to her new home, calculating how to get back there by the fastest and most efficient route. I imagined my flat in London, empty and waiting, a dusty museum to the person I used to be, it felt like it belonged to another life, a different girl.

When the weather finally broke I waited all day by the port but boat after boat was cancelled anyway for reasons I didn't understand. Eventually as dusk fell I found a car ferry that would take me back to the mainland. 'Better after than never!' said the cheery Croatian man who'd been waiting with me all day.

As the ferry made its slow way across the dark sea I thought about searching and returning, about love and its endurance, about the grief I kept pushing away every time I talked to my father, the way I modulated my voice when we spoke so he couldn't tell how sad I was, how I could never tell him what I really felt because it would just be a howl. I thought about the slightness of the connections made on the road and how they seemed to hold, that on Korčula I'd found three women who had shown me three different ways of being.

Zagreb airport in the too-cold of early December looked like a budget sci-fi film, empty and overlit with rows of abandoned check-in desks and just one woman sitting alone behind all the counters, reading *Jane Eyre*. She put it down reluctantly to pick up my passport.

I was on my way to an island where one-eyed monsters were said to roam, and getting there would be complex, new PCR tests had been introduced and the clock was ticking. I got on to a plane exhausted from holding the tension of it. I tried not to breathe.

Chapter Eight

Island of the Cyclopes

Menorca, Spain

Strangers! Who are you? Where did you come from
across the watery depths? Are you on business,
or roaming around without a goal, like pirates

The Cyclops

So did his eyeball crackle on the spear.
Horribly then he howled, the rocks resounded

The sky was the brightest of winter blues above the yellow town of Mahón. All the buildings were painted shades of citrus and lemon, ochre and mustard and every hue in between. Palm trees rattled in the wind and the road swept down the hill towards the deep port where white yachts waited, in their superior, gleaming way, for summer.

Along the central shopping avenue orange trees were still bursting with fruit and sparrows gathered on their branches at dusk to scream the day's news at each other, their volume increasing as the light fell, until at twilight the chatter crescendoed so loudly you had to raise your voice to be heard over it. After the bone cold of icy Zagreb, it felt tropical here by comparison, the air warmer and softer. I had won an extra hour of light, the days stretched open in front of me again, there was sunshine optimism spinning through these yellow streets.

In one of my favourite children's books, *The Tiger Who Came to Tea*, the cafe is the hero, fixes everything, makes everybody happy, restores order. I was newly thankful for cafes being open again in a world raided by tigers, as I sat high on the green terrace of Cafe Nou overlooking the orange trees with their sparrows, eating a *tostada con tomate* and reading about Mauricio Obregón. He was a twentieth-century historian and university professor who spent a lot of his time retracing ancient voyages. He believed that the island of the Cyclops could be one of the Balearic Islands – so the land where one-eyed monsters used to roam might be here, on Menorca.

In the story, Poseidon has an affair with a sea-nymph who immediately gets pregnant – no god ever has issues with sperm count – and their child grows up to become the strongest of all the Cyclopes, and lives a quiet life on an island as a shepherd.

After a narrow escape from the lures of psychedelic plant medicine in the land of the Lotus Eaters, and after barbequing goats on the 'island full of wonders', Odysseus and twelve of his men set out on an expedition to find the Cyclops. They break into his cave, wait for the monster to come home and, when he does, in yet another classic example of poor judgement, Odysseus demands a gift, per the guest-code protocol. The Cyclops, unsurprisingly, declines to give a present to the home intruders. Instead he traps them and snacks on some of the crew, in between nipping out to graze his sheep. Odysseus, wily as ever, forms a plan, gets the monster blind drunk, shoves a sharpened stick into his eye, and manages to escape with the remainder of the uneaten crew.

Once they're safely back on the ship he arrogantly taunts the blinded giant. Infuriated, the monster chucks an enormous rock at the ship, but misses, obviously, since he can't see. Enraged, the Cyclops turns to daddy for help.

> Listen, Earth-Shaker, Blue-Haired Lord Poseidon:
> acknowledge me your son, and be my father.
> Grant that Odysseus, the city-sacker,
> will never go back home

In response, 'Lord Poseidon rages, unrelenting.' A vengeful god now has a personal vendetta. Smart move, Odysseus.

I rented an apartment where black smoke came out of the plug sockets and lamps exploded, shattering glass everywhere, but it was cheap and central. I needed to find a bicycle but both the hire shops in town quoted astronomical prices – a week's rental was more than a bike would cost to buy in London, and I couldn't just buy one here because the only ones for sale were the high-end type that Lycra-people use and cost thousands of pounds. Without a bike I was stuck, the water at the port was too oily and polluted for swimming, and it was too far to walk to the nearest beach. When I said I'd become addicted to cold water I mean this in a very real way: my body had become dependent, and I was starting to feel on edge after a whole week in Mahón without swimming. I wondered about hiring a car, it seemed unnecessary, although the real reason was an uncharacteristic lack of confidence.

Five years ago, just after he was diagnosed, my father had an operation that gutted him like an animal to cut out as much cancer as possible. It wasn't curative but it would slow everything down, and he spent a week in hospital recovering. It was November, or at least it feels November-ish in my memory, cold and dark too early, and all the roads icy and dangerous. I'd just driven back to the house when he demanded I turn around and come back to the hospital with some new underwear.

'Can it wait until tomorrow?'

'No, it bloody can't,' he snapped.

I was tired to my depths, experiencing a weightedness that was more than physical. It was the kind of emotional exhaustion my body would have to try and get used to in the slow-mo years that followed, but at that moment everything was still new and overwhelming. I called my mother who was in the hospital with him. 'Do I have to come in? I'm so tired.'

'I know, darling, but he really wants new underwear,' she said. What he really wanted, I think, was control, and he was projecting it on to a pair of boxers, but anyway, I got the car out of the garage again and drove back down the black slippery roads, retracing myself. I was crossing a roundabout when a car drove into the side of me. At least that's what it felt like. The insurance company determined later that it was my fault. The other driver was shaken and polite and we both kept apologising to each other. I called my father, didn't want to alarm him, worded it carefully.

'I've had a bit of a prang, I'm okay but your car isn't.'

Immediately, he cheered up, became an automobile insurance specialist, told me to do all the things I'd already done, and some other stuff that I would never have thought of doing.

'I'm sorry about your pants, Dad.'

'Don't worry about it!' he said happily, sounding like his old self again. The car crash was better than new underwear, more transformative, the collision turning him back into a father instead of a post-operative patient, gave him something else to focus on. I told him not to tell my brother who'd be mean about it forever. I'm not normally avoidant but after this I became more careful about driving. Anyway, I didn't want to hire a car here. I wanted a bicycle.

In a tapas bar I was saying all this to the bartender. A practised therapist, he put a beer and olives in front of me as he listened.

'Oh, you can just take my bike,' said a woman sitting on the stool at the end of the bar, 'I'll get it from my sister's house for you and bring it tomorrow.'

'But you don't even know me!'

Montese silenced this objection by simply introducing herself, and with that the old island magic started to flow again. The next day, good as her word, she wheeled an old bicycle up the street towards the bar – flat tires, a rusty chain and wonky brakes, but all easily fixed. I had wheels again, was free again. She refused to accept any money so I left flowers for her. 'Island generosity,' my father

166

marvelled when I told him, but I was less surprised, more used by now to how kind strangers could be. 'People obviously like you,' he said, 'you're obviously good at meeting people and they give you bikes and invite you for meals.'

I puffed a little, he rarely gave praise.

'I just wish you'd be more like that with the family, we rarely see that side of you,' he said. I should have seen it coming, he was a master of the backhanded compliment. Critical and loving all mixed up together. Having terminal cancer doesn't automatically make you into a saint. Equally, it didn't turn me into one either, I sniped back at him.

In London the bike journey to and from places was often the part I enjoyed most, the anticipation of getting to a party, the relief of riding away from it, freewheeling through dark streets flashing red and white lights towards home, roads spinning under my tires, weaving through the traffic, light and unstoppable against the density of the city, down towpaths alongside the darkly rippling water wondering if I toppled in, whether I could save my bike and myself. Fast up and over Tower Bridge, London Bridge, Blackfriars, slowly along the Embankment at night under the strings of fairy lights, dolphins curving tightly around each other at the base of each lamp post, and the river water brash with flickering pink and blue lights from the theatres on the opposite bank. My glide paths, shortcuts, the quickest ways home through the dark and the cold and the rain. The longer ways for when it was sunny, or I was nervous, the bicycle movement bringing me back to myself.

I cycled on Montese's bike around the island and found rocky coves to swim in. On my rides I saw birds everywhere, moving through the air like musical notes, folding their wings mid-flight to drop and bounce. White, cloud-high birds flew in circles above me as I biked to the sea, black and white birds with long tails hopped along the lanes, flying up just in time as I rode past. Tiny birds moved between the low branches of olive trees, heads cocked, eyes blinking, regarding each other, and me. I became entranced, obsessive, almost. This was a language I wanted to learn.

Javier, a Menorcan ornithologist, became my translator. I'd booked a 'bird walking tour' but there was no one else on it, just me. Javier was tall with dark hair and a shy smile, he wore serious hiking trousers, a rucksack with a proper chest fastening, had two pairs of binoculars looped around his neck, and carried a telescope over his shoulder. He looked precisely like an ornithologist should look, not that I'd ever seen one before. I liked him immediately.

We drove to the wetland behind Son Bou, a sandy beach on the south coast, and watched through binoculars as a marsh hawk prowled for a distracted duck to pounce on. Marsh hawks drown ducks by standing on their heads before eating them, Javier told me, and the duck's only defensive strategy is to keep an eye on the skies above them, and dive deep if they spy a hawk.

Our next stop was a meadow where small birds were feasting on thistle seeds, Javier set up the telescope and identified with scientific accuracy each of the feathered messengers of the gods, teaching me their names in Spanish, Catalan and English – which frankly was too much information, I stopped him when he started trying to tell me their Latin names too. It turned out that birds spend far longer on the ground looking for food than I'd realised, naively imagining them to be mostly in flight or singing in trees. With Javier I was learning the toddler-like pleasure of precision-naming things, of knowing what the different birds were called, where they lived, what they liked to eat. I wrote down all the facts, ready to impress Theo who was obsessed with the natural world. Flashy goldfinches and showy greenfinches nominate sentries to watch and warn of predators while the rest of the flock feed in the fields. Robins are called *ropit* in Catalan, and female blackcaps actually have brown caps, it's only the males that sport black ones. When booted eagles in white feathered trousers circle and call in their strangely thin voices, touching feathers, they're actually spinning courtship through the sky, going on joyride love flights together. Those huge white birds I'd seen flying through clouds were 'the Egyptians' in Javier's lexicon. He meant Egyptian vultures. They looked ugly and ancient and reptilian up close when he showed me a picture of them in his Collins bird book, but they looked beautiful flying white through the sky, a ring of black wing feathers framing their underbodies. The lazy Egyptian Vultures don't bother hunting, they just patrol the sides of the roads, looking for carrion to feast on.

As we walked through the woods, Javier untangled birdsong into individual melodies for me, ascribing singers to particular notes. We never saw the Cetti's warbler, a shy brown bird easily camouflaged, but Javier taught me to distinguish his song as he sang from between the trees, loud, abrupt and distinctive. He told me that the hoopoe was the iconic bird of Menorca and I could see why, it looked like a rebel spirit with an orange punk-rock mohican, swirling polka-dot wings, and a looping butterfly flight, although my favourite of the birds he showed me that day was the small Sardinian warbler, puff-plump and joyful.

We drove up to the north coast where Javier pointed out a blue rock thrush flying near the sea cliffs. It was about the size of a starling and all its feathers were the perfect shade of imaginary blue, it looked like Disney. Soon, he told me, the scent of camomile flowers will fill the air along the trail and bright bee-eaters will return from Africa, along with pink flamingos and other migrant birds, to feast on mosquitoes all summer long.

Alongside knowing everything there was to know about birds,
Javier was also a dab hand at 'catching' slender stems of wild asparagus
while we walked. At the end of our long day together I cooked them
and savoured the intense, almost spicy taste of the woods.

Happiness came down to this: a bicycle, low-walled narrow country
lanes to slow-cycle down, a turquoise sea cradled by a rocky cove,
a bright day, and a notebook so I could write down the new things
I'd learned to see. Black redstarts, a pair of kestrels, speckled wood
butterflies, a dormouse rustling up a tree, a poison-caterpillar
nest, a red kite flashing rust through the air. And try to capture
something about the smell of the heat inside the sandy pinewoods,
or the shape of the sculptures of the sea, which bleached driftwood
sand-coloured before arranging it on winter beaches with a curator's
eye. I missed almost nothing about London. Here I was in constant
motion, cycling to the sea, finding donkeys in small green fields,
watching the birds, thinking and not thinking about my father.
I was becoming more animal, more feathered, more creature.

My mother visited Menorca fifty years ago when she was nineteen.
She'd never been abroad before and came with her best friend. The
two girls flirted with a rugby team in the hotel pool during the

endless hot days, and at night competed to win a bottle of cheap champagne by throwing a hoop over the neck.

'All we did all day was laugh and laugh,' she said, the sunburned nineteen-year-old girl whirling in her voice, she's young again, and dreaming.

'I guess the cheap wine had something to do with that.'

'I always said I'd go back,' she said, longing traced with sadness, the way people speak when they never truly believe they'll return to a place. 'It's such a beautiful island.'

I wanted her to tell me more, asked for the names of the beaches she remembered going to, wrote them all down and visited them for her, writing her name in the sand.

I moved out of my apartment to a small summer house near the village of Sant Lluís in the south of the island. It felt good to be out of the bustle of Mahón and the quiet countryside around the village reminded me of home. Many islanders have a *casa de campo* like this, a second home in the countryside that they move to in the summer to be cooler, away from the town. Lent by a generous friend of a friend, this summer house originally belonged to someone who worked in fashion, and was stylishly put together, whitewashed walls, white sheepskin rugs flung on snow-white sofas, diagonal blue and yellow slanted tiles up the central staircase, cathedral-like arches in all the rooms, red floors, a wood-burning stove, and a garden full of trees and birds, surrounded by farmland. The cottage came complete with her mother, a chic French lady who was staying out of Paris for the same reason I didn't want to go back to London. It was beautiful here and life started to hold a rhythm and a shape again. Being in a different home, another house, is a way of testing out being a different person. I was less agitated and scratchy, less clawsome. This wasn't my house, it belonged to someone else, but living here felt next door to home somehow.

My favourite place at the summer house was the outdoor table in the garden. I swaddled myself in jumpers and breakfasted there daily, eating a bowl of strawberries, or two cooling boiled eggs with a piece of French bread, or a sweet tart from the bakery, and looked out at the garden, fat with birdsong. Sardinian warblers jumped through the branches of the olive trees flashing their white chests, cocking their black heads and regarding me with their mystical red bird-eyes. Then I'd work for a few hours – the company had started by asking me to look at market innovation and how best to capture new opportunities, and this had extended into putting a business case together to set up a new strategic alliances team. I built decks, checked assumptions, spoke each day to the woman who led their strategy division, and the team who did mergers and acquisitions, before cycling to the sea to swim at lunchtime, returning with frozen hands to make a hot water bottle and strap it against my stomach in the unheated house to thaw out again and work some more. In the evenings I'd cycle to the field where three donkeys lived, or wander down the lanes before the light gave out. All those well-being gurus talk about the importance of a routine. Finding a rhythm, making rituals, I think is part of feeling at home.

I was rushing one day, to squeeze in a short swim between meetings and not paying enough attention in my sea lust. I saw a dead jellyfish on a rock and looked at it with grim satisfaction but the wind was in the right direction so I didn't bother to do a proper scan of the sea, jumped straight into the water and was punished by *medusa* for my carelessness. I could never quite get used to being stung, it always took a few seconds for my brain to figure out what the watery, shock-whipping feeling was, to translate it, and this one felt especially electrical. When I got back to the house I realised how bad the stings were, my whole leg felt hot. As I was examining it, my father called.

'The latest treatment hasn't worked as well as we'd hoped…'

My father's way of speaking, his cadence, involved pausing for long periods in the middle of a sentence – people often thought he had lost his train of thought, but it was just habit, and nothing would rush him, you simply had to wait until he started up again. Perhaps it was partly the legacy of his training, the way they teach doctors to communicate, so that patients can try and absorb the information in the white spaces in between letters and sounds, take it in in the gaps. He was speaking more slowly than normal, and this pause lasted longer, stretched out.

'… the cancer has become more aggressive. It didn't start out that way but cancers can sometimes do that,' he said with detached clinical precision, employing his best bedside manner on himself.

My turn to pause. I looked at the floorboards, at the yellow light streaming in from the street lamp, the reverse shadow of the windowpanes on the floor. He'd told me it would kill him one day but it had been treated, zapped, held in abeyance by different combinations of drugs, each one 'holding the line' until it didn't any longer, but then the doctors would start something new, there was always something new to try. That's the thing with end-stage cancer, it's this sort of endless calibration and recalibration of hope, not for a cure, but for more time, and as each treatment line fails, hope gets weighed and measured again, gets reaffirmed, because what's the alternative? This, I think, is what people mean when they talk of the cruelty of terminal diseases.

'How are you feeling?' I asked. It was always hard to tell, he never spoke of his feelings. Our currency was always jokes, never emotions.

'I feel deeply sad about it. I feel sad for your mother. But we'll "storm heaven" as they'd say in Dublin. There's one last throw of the dice, one final treatment option. I wish I had better news to give you, my darling daughter.'

'Your body is doing its best.' I was keeping my voice steady, writing down what he was saying so I could reread it, so I had a transcript, so I wouldn't need to ask him to repeat himself. I understood that without the drugs controlling it, the cancer was no longer stable, like it was when I left, it could become volatile, it was at risk of growing unchecked. 'At least you can stop taking those chemo pills over Christmas.' My forced cheer didn't ring right.

'I hated taking that poison. I *hated* those tablets.'

I made noises that were supposed to mean: I love you, I'm sorry, I don't know what to say. Sounds are less reliable than words but more capacious, they stretch, become whatever you need them to mean.

'I'm sad for all my children, I'm sad I haven't responded better to the treatment. How are you?'

I let him swerve. You can come close to sadness and you need to move away from it again. We composed a reply to an email I'd been struggling to write, precision tweezed words together. It was trivial, it didn't matter, but it was what he wanted to do.

'Can I do anything?' It sounded awkward when I said it, that's the other thing with cancer, there's not much you can actually do, it makes you useless, helpless, howling.

'I don't think so, sweetheart. You call and we have these little chats and that's nice.' How slight that felt when he said it, how flimsy, 'these little chats'.

I wished I'd made that podcast with him, it could have been a way to give him an audience, he liked to perform. I should have been nicer about a video he'd recorded in lockdown, he'd sent it to me sweetly wondering if perhaps it would go viral? 'Too long,' I'd said, brutally, 'not funny enough.' I wished I'd recorded all our conversations, I wanted to pin him like a moth in a museum display case, to capture it all before it went, before something in him slowed and stopped.

'I've been lucky to have two of the best consultants in my corner.' He often said how lucky he felt, and there was a grace in it. 'When are you coming home, sweetheart?'

At this point restrictions were changing almost every week, Spain had banned UK arrivals, there were rumours that England would add Spain to its 'red list'. It was impossible to plan.

'Maybe in March.' There was a pause.

'Well, sweetheart, your mother would love to see you before March.'

I didn't pay attention to that tiny caesura, the semicolon, a moment of stillness. I skim-read a pause. I missed the repetition of 'sweetheart'. I'll go back to this moment again and again later, when I'm trying to make sense of everything. Perhaps I was in denial, not hearing properly, seeing with one eye. It's hard to listen to what sits underneath the words. It's hard to hear abstraction.

'Last time I saw you, you made me climb a ladder to my bedroom!' I was trying to lift the mood, this had been back in the summer when it had been legal for me to visit but he'd been paranoid and didn't want me walking through the house. 'If I had slipped we'd have much bigger worries than covid.'

'Well, you still can't come inside, I'm afraid, I have to minimise risk.'

It was my time to swerve, I told him how I got lashed by a jellyfish and a massive area all around my thigh was raised and the skin had gone bumpy and blistered because of the sting concentration – it must have wrapped around my leg, I said, or maybe several of them attacked together in a pack.

Focusing on this physical pain enabled him to be a doctor again. He wanted to see a photograph, made me wait on the line while he researched. 'It's probably an allergic reaction and it will get worse the more you're stung, you have to be more careful. Go to the chemist and get some hydrocortisone cream.'

'Okay, Dad,' I said. A clinical way of prescribing love but I understood what he was trying to say as we both focused on the jellyfish, something that could be fixed, treated, resolved. I would heal, get better, be well again.

After we said goodbye I sat on the floor for a long time, my stings itch-burning, throat thickened, until I realised I was starting to shiver, my body was shaking and I was thirsty and deeply tired. I wished he didn't know, didn't have to give these updates about what wasn't working. Everyone was suffering in the pandemic. At least I was here. I'm lucky I'm lucky I'm lucky, I repeated like a mantra, tracing my fingers across my swollen leg to soothe the hot stings, now a red concentrated mass, practically glowing. I thought about calling my brother or Rachel or Katharine or my friend Pella but my stomach swirled and pulled sharply down. I started vomiting and I couldn't stop, opening my mouth obediently for my body. How easily I was weakened, made to crawl.

As my body cramped and fought the poison over the next two days I thought about Medusa again. In every version of the story it all ends the same way: her hair turns snake, her eyes turn men to stone, her skin turns poison. Scientists have found that some jellyfish are biologically immortal, they can revert to an earlier stage of their life cycle. Unlike us, they can start again.

Three days later, wobbling-weak like unsteady Bambi, I walked slowly through blazing white wintery sunlight for Christmas lunch at the Hotel Jardí de Ses Bruixes. It was the sort of place I imagined Scott and Zelda Fitzgerald staying, a kind of old-fashioned Riviera glamour. I took a table in the walled garden under a lemon tree, wrapping myself in hotel blankets against the slight December-ish cold. I'd called ahead to say I'd been unwell and wasn't sure if I could manage the full menu. I arrived to find that the chef had designed a whole new set of dishes specifically to soothe my empty, tenderised stomach. I almost cried at the kindness, pulled myself together. 'Oh come let us adore him!' sang quietly from the speakers. What a year it had been. The opposite of god is a jellyfish. And the next best thing to love is paying to be looked after.

We'd had a Zoom call Christmas earlier that day but it hadn't worked very well, my father looked tired, my brother was stressed, Theo was bored and disruptive, his new baby sister Willow had just been born and was stealing the limelight. There hadn't been much festive cheer even though everyone had been trying to make an effort.

'It's a little chilly outside, would madame like to take her dessert by the fire?' The tree standing in the lobby on the way to the drawing room was perfectly decorated, sparkling fairy lights and hand-carved wooden decorations in reds and greens. I stood looking at it for long moments. My favourite part of Christmas is decorating the tree, is transformations.

In the green striped drawing room I was greeted by Alma, a golden retriever with movie-star looks and a festive red bow. Francesca, her glamorous Italian owner, in her fifties, immaculately dressed with a perfect manicure and an enormous diamond necklace, had a house on the island and a fashion business in Milan. We sat talking by the blazing fire, Francesca bought me a drink and invited me to tea the next day. Alma came and lay down at my feet, curling up against me like we were old friends.

Christmas alone, and all at once I wasn't alone at all.

Chapter Nine

Land of the Cimmerians

Menorca, Spain

I wanted to embrace
The spirit of my mother. She was dead,
and I did not know how. Three times I tried,
longing to touch her. But three times her ghost
flew from my arms, like shadows or like dreams

Odysseus

'You're the most ungrateful person in the world,' my father was shouting down the phone.

I didn't know how we'd ended up here, fallen into the old grooves of the old resentments, caught in the beats of the argument that was never about what it was really about. Back in the usual stuck places, my father demanding gratitude for a private education at a school where I became unhappy, where I learned that even the parts of a person you wouldn't think could get any smaller can, that even the tiny flesh between finger knuckles can shrink to the bone. 'You can't just tell a person to feel the emotions you want them to feel.' I was yelling back. We'd always been equally matched, he and I. 'I'm sick of your cancer. There's no space for me, I'm alone in this stupid pandemic, I'm scared about the future and it's all cancer cancer cancer.'

Rage hot on my face, guilt bloating my stomach. I should be a better daughter but he should be a better father. I was wheeling my bike, the better to argue because he'd complained about the wind noise when I tried to use my headset.

'You can't have a fair fight with a cancer patient.'

'That's true darling. I can see that. I am very sorry about that.' He shifted, softened, but it was too late. I got to the summer house, crashed the bike against the wall, locked it, stomped inside. I shouldn't have said anything. Well, he shouldn't have provoked me. I snapped and hung up, got into bed wearing all my clothes and shivered in the summer house winter cold, weeping like one of those stupid girls in the stories. Useless, sad, boneless girls waiting to be rescued, waiting so long they fall asleep for a million years before a prince braves thorns and witches to save them from all the wickedness in the world. I am all thorn, all witch. When I woke up, I saw he'd sent a big red heart over WhatsApp, the huge one, the one that beats. All these 'I love you's, pictures of hearts, swift forgiveness, it wasn't like him. He was becoming more and more unlike himself. It was a transition I wanted to reverse, claw back. I wanted my real father back, the one who would never say this in a million years, the one who liked to point out my 'flaws and foibles' in forensic detail. When we spoke again later and apologised to each other, he told me that I was like him.

The wind was coming from the north, a strong tramontana wind, the worst kind. It had been building all day and now it deepened and shook around the house. Windstorms in Menorca are immersive events. Staying inside doesn't help much and if you go outside the wind gets into your ears and makes you sick, gets into your body and exhausts you in a unique way that's difficult to explain if you haven't felt the endlessness of it. It felt relentless, like being slammed inside a migraine or a compression headache. There was pressure and negative sound and it seemed to affect all the fluids in my body. There was no escape, nothing to do but wait it out. The storms build and often last for days. The palm trees were shaking outside and plastic sheeting somewhere was flapping, and everything inside me seemed under siege, and the whole world uncertain, tremulous, fragile. I willed myself back to sleep but lay there in the cold bed with my eyes closed, awake and angry, resentful and remorseful all at once, listening to the wind whipping across the island, desolate and cold.

The land of the Cimmerians, shrouded by mist and clouds, is where the spirits of the dead wander. Odysseus follows Circe's instructions and performs a ritual to call them to him, in order to seek guidance from a dead prophet called Tiresias about how to make it home safely. He pours libations, sprinkles some barley on top, and fills a hole with the 'black blood' of a couple of sacrificial sheep for the dead to drink. Slowly, ghosts begin to appear, including some of the fallen soldiers of the Trojan war who fought alongside him. Most of them have some kind of post-traumatic stress syndrome, unsurprisingly, and they 'spoke in tears'. When the shade of his mother appears, Odysseus attempts to embrace her but she slips through his arms. He tries again, and again. I thought a lot about this 'failed hug' later. It haunted me.

My father didn't like touching people, was extremely paranoid about germs for a doctor. If he caught a cold he'd attribute it furiously to the person he decided to blame and this would go on for long months afterwards – I've got your brother's bug or your mother's cold, he'd rage and lament. It's a wonder he went into medicine. Instead of a hug, our greeting ritual was to pat each other's backs with increasing force and velocity until it turned into hard slaps and stopped only when one of us couldn't stand it any more. Love and brutality all at once. He was raised in the 1950s and sent young to boarding school. I guess affection was withdrawn early for him – I have to guess because he rarely spoke about his parents or his childhood. He had lost his own father when he was seventeen, and said, when talking about the perfect dinner party, that he would choose for his guest his own dad. He said he'd like to get to know him better, and something about this caught behind my eyes.

It was New Year's Eve. I cycled down to the sea near the village of Alcaufar on the south coast and eased myself into the seaweed-strewn water, wondering if the cold could offset anything any more, if there was any point to this daily baptism into the depths and the deep, if the new year would bring any changes. I saw three hoopoe birds as I cycled back up the hill on ice-numb feet, and noticed that there was something uncertain, something wobbly, about the way they flew through the air, an erratic pattern. A cat cried out or maybe it was a chicken. I biked on to Biniparratx. The sign promised a cove at the end of a ravine – I imagined a sharp, deep drop, a place where people might lose their footing and tumble, or be pushed. A place where cars could fall down off mountain roads. But when I got there it was just an exaggerated translation, the place was more of a shallow gully. Birds whirled and screamed about the cliffs which, the same sign had said, were dotted with Bronze Age burial chambers. I climbed up and sat high in the sun watching the thrashing of the disturbed sea.

That evening I learned that the Spanish custom is to eat a grape for every strike of the clock at midnight. I tried and choked, mouth full like a hamster, eyes watering.

My father refused to talk about his Catholic faith, it was a private thing between him and his God, no need for me to be involved, but I had lost my own faith and I wanted to find my way to his. Although I had broken with the church, discarded the religion young and early, the guilt it was infused with has proved harder to remove. I was curious about his beliefs, asked him many times, straight on and slantways, and he never answered, got irritated, finally said 'I just don't want to talk about it' in the old sharp tone that was a warning. A doctor, a man of science, a person oriented to rational above emotional, who weighed evidence, calibrated medications, joined dots between data points, still believed in the mystery, still went to church and increased the frequency of his attendance after he was diagnosed. I knew there were relics in his sock drawer, chips of a saint's tooth, supposedly, or perhaps a piece of bone, a splinter of wood, possibly purporting to be from the cross, it was unclear. They were in small white jewellery boxes with transparent plastic covers, carefully packed, the cotton wool yellowing. There was an old rosary in there as well. Sometimes when I was taking his socks (unauthorised), I lifted it out, ran my hands across the heavy beads. I didn't know how he'd got these things.

I did know he'd visited Lourdes as a child on a sort of pilgrimage but the details were hazy, I'm not sure why he was taken there. Perhaps it had to do with the mild polio he'd had – as a child he'd worn a leather back brace and, regardless of this correction, he retained a slight scoliosis of the spine, suffered from a bad back. Or maybe it was just a school trip. When I'd told him about climbing the volcano on Aeolus's island, how spiritual it felt, the torches of other walkers glowing in the dark like candles, he'd mentioned Lourdes then, said he'd found it very moving, then clammed up, that was all he wanted to say. After the shock of the original diagnosis had slowed, had changed into something wider and brighter from its initial sharp point, we talked about the *Camino de Santiago*. He'd wanted to walk it, and it seemed like the right time to go, I'd said, imagining the two of us and that beautiful old saint who walked with so many on that ancient road.

Walking was always our thing, the two of us in the countryside in Oxfordshire, mostly not talking, just being alongside each other. I'd tell him difficult things sometimes, and he'd listen or tell me long-winded allegorical stories, or remind me of road trips a million years ago in Ireland with my second cousin Una and her husband Jack, trying to make me laugh. I tried again to get him to commit to dates for the *Camino* and he never said no outright, but it never quite materialised either. I think he didn't want to leave my mother.

Eventually I stopped asking. Perhaps I should have pushed harder. The rules for cancer are not clear. Then he needed to stay near the hospital for the treatments, and the *Camino* remained unwalked. Walking was pretty much the only time I spent alone with him. The times he seemed to see me most clearly, as a person. Other times, especially in my early childhood, I was less visible to him. On the last walk he'd been telling me a story about a patient of his who had committed suicide. How sad he was about it. How he attended the funeral, sitting at the back.

Walking has always shaken my mind clear of spinning thoughts, transmuted half-formed, half-felt feelings into concrete ones: tiredness, strain and stretch, let my muscles take over, my mind go blank and sideways, laterally into the soundscape, stretching itself into the silence, into the quiet, extending towards beauty and away from the smallness of my concerns.

Walking all the way around Menorca didn't start as a pilgrimage, at least not consciously, although perhaps a part of me was searching for a way to make a repair, to atone, to fix all the arguments forever, to make an offering to the gods. I wanted to walk because I needed to gather my thoughts. It wasn't clear to me what to do next, whether to fly home or to stay. Spain had locked out UK arrivals but there was a way back if I needed to find one. But what use would I be there? In my mother's words, there was nothing I could do. Everything felt heavy and wrong. My mind whirred, weighing options. The right thing isn't always obvious at the time, although it glows brightly in retrospect, indelible in hindsight. It was only afterwards that I realised this walk was something devotional. It was only afterwards that I realised I should have returned home sooner.

There's a costal path that runs all the way around the island called the *Camí de Cavalls*. I stumbled over the trail by accident one day when I was visiting a new beach, and followed the cherry-red signposts for a while. The next day I bought a map and started hiking sections every chance I got.

This path was created by Iberian King James II in the fourteenth century to improve Menorca's defences – islanders had to keep an armoured horse on standby and patrol along its length. The *Camí* wasn't much help though – the island was almost constantly under attack from pirates, most notably in 1535, when famously bloodthirsty Barbarossa sacked the city of Mahón, capturing more than six hundred islanders, and dragging them back to Algiers as slaves. Then in the eighteenth century the place was repeatedly invaded by European powers, who valued its strategic position at the heart of the Mediterranean.

I walked for hours along the sandy path high above the flashing kingfisher-coloured coast, through hot pine forests and along clifftops. I walked accompanied by the soft music of cow bells. I hiked until my legs ached and then plunged into icy water and lay out to dry in the indifferent spring sunshine. Spring came early to the island and the green was the most intense I'd ever seen. The blossom was already given over to fresh greening leaves as I walked, another shade of green against all the green.

I passed through empty villages of second houses built as close to the water as possible and as I walked and as the weather warmed, I started to notice a sudden flurry of activity, of gardening and construction to repair the worst of the salt erosions. Things were being newly painted glitter white, ready for summer.

As I walked I noticed the geology changing drastically, something I'd never paid much attention to before. On the wild north coast, I passed what looked like a parody of the English countryside, verdant green fields and leafy trees. I walked through extravagant red clover and big optimistic daisies in the south, trying to ignore warning signs about enormous bees, and explored abandoned beach bunkers dug to defend against Franco, the Spanish dictator. In the end they weren't used, Franco invaded by air and punished Menorca's opposition, by holding islanders on prison ships for years, and by denying the island development funding. I passed by old Spanish- and English-built watchtowers as alternating powers constructed new fortifications. The path took me to a paleo-Christian basilica in ruins, where there was ancient Greek graffiti on the stones. I sat on the hilltop with my back against the ruins eating *pastissets*, a biscuit a bit like shortbread, watching two booted eagles surfing the thermals, calling to each other, weaving geometric love poetry between their wing tips. I walked to shining Mitjana beach and sliced through emerald waters to reach its sister, tiny Mitjaneta, around the headland, where I wrote my mother's name on the sand. I wanted to think about her and not my father for a change. I wanted to picture her lying on the sand in her stripy bikini young and happy and sunburned.

In the east I walked to Cala Rafalet where tall cliffs framed a narrow stretch of blue sea. The way to reach it felt like a secret, the path twisting down through a dark green forest to a deep ravine, where shimmering light-green rock pools cascaded into each other, and finally opened on to a narrow azure swimming stretch where the shadowed water was so cold it made me gasp. I walked barefoot on white silk beaches on the southern coast and over coarser, coral-pink sand on the northern coast which was even more fervently, evangelically green than in the south, and where tiny whitewashed fishermen's huts clung to the sides of isolated small coves, each one an even more idyllic version of a house by the sea than the last.

My father called as I walked to tell me about his port insert, an opening made inside him so they could give him medicine more easily. Something swelled in my chest and burst. I willed him here, wanted to airlift him out, wanted more than anything for him to be walking next to me, well again. All I could do was describe it for him. He suggested I write an article. 'People would be interested,' he said, 'about how you're doing the pandemic differently, my brilliant daughter.' I brushed it off, said I didn't know how, but promised him I'd try and find out.

At Cales Coves, a double cove on the south coast, I walked into a Bronze Age necropolis, a great city for the dead. One hundred burial chambers were carved high into the cliffs by the mysterious prehistoric Talayotic civilisation. Their dead were given amazing sea views and they were never lonely – laid to rest in communal graves, chiselled out by hand.

Down by the water a woman was stripping off her wetsuit. I liked how Menorcans were completely unselfconscious about being stark naked. As I changed into my swimming stuff next to her we started talking. She told me these caves had been occupied by hippies, and she had grown up in one of them. 'My mother gave birth to her last two children in the cave, with just my father, and the neighbour with a knife,' she laughed. 'Can you imagine?' They lived amongst the dead in what became a popular alternative commune until the Spanish authorities kicked them all out and boarded up most of the caves.

I slowly lowered myself into the deep water trying not to shriek, not wanting her to judge me novice. Halfway across to the other shore, I caught my breath when a kingfisher flashed towards me. The bird was almost too fast to follow, a neon line, an electric, buzzing movement. 'Did you see that?' I called over, and she gave me a thumbs up from the shore. She'd seen my bird, it was real. Finally, there was someone to share this magic with. We flashed grins at each other across the water. This was the third time Aeolus had sent his daughter to me on my travels.

Aeolus, ruler of the winds, had a beautiful daughter, Alcyone. She isn't in *The Odyssey* like her father, but her story is worth telling. A Thessalian princess, she made a starry marriage, quite literally, exchanging vows with Ceyx, son of the morning star. They fast became one of those annoyingly blissful couples. They were also a little kinky and enjoyed role play in bed, calling each other 'Zeus' and 'Hera', but this sacrilegious pillow talk cost them their happily ever after. When he heard about it, Zeus was enraged – he was nothing if not laser-focused on the smallest of microaggressions, and quick to take offence in the ways of gods. True to vengeful form, he immediately threw a thunderbolt at the ship Ceyx was on, killing him instantly. When she learned of his death, Alcyone threw herself into the sea, killing herself in a paroxysm of grief, such was her sea-deep love for her husband. Unpredictable Zeus, touched by this act of love, turned compassionate and decided to reincarnate the lovers as a pair of kingfishers.

Legend tells that kingfishers lay their eggs on the surface of the sea in mid-December while Alcyone's father keeps the winds quiet. In reality, they dig a tunnel in the riverbank and lay their eggs underground. Unlike with most birds, the female has the brightest feathers. After I was finished swimming and jumping up and down to warm up, I looked up the symbology. Kingfishers are associated with freedom, courage and adventure. They assist with letting go, and with forward movement. I needed to let go, to move on, but if you let things go, what takes their place?

My phone pinged – now Rachel had a beautiful daughter too. In the photograph, my friend looked fierce and tired and happy. The birth had been complicated. She had been brave. The baby would be named after Lady Hester Stanhope, a famous explorer. It was perfect. I sent kisses across the airways to my friend, to her longed-for child.

When the *Camí* cut along the south it went through little valleys of low stone walls that mosaicked tiny fields and ran alongside flower meadows, pastures with grazing horses, orchards and patches of wild olives. But in the west the landscape shifted. There were no pine or oak forests on this side of the island, instead it looked like something out of *Wuthering Heights*: bleak, windswept rocks and lines of dry stone walls and round stone huts for sheep to shelter in. I tied my jumper over my ears as the northern tramontane wind that shaped this landscape roared around my head as I walked past an iron cross at the top of a sheer cliff commemorating a shipwreck.

As I walked for hours alone on the trail, or with Francesca, my friend from Christmas, and her dog Alma, my mind misted and cleared. Who knew what this shifting-sand world would bring next, but for now at least there was a path to follow, a section of the map to tick off.

By February my circumnavigation of the island was three-quarters complete and it was my father's birthday. He was reading *A Time of Gifts* by Patrick Leigh Fermor, a memoir of the time Patrick had spent walking as a pilgrim from Holland to Germany in 1933 when he was eighteen years old. *Lots of parallels with your experience*, he texted, *particularly the hospitality he experienced even in Germany at the time when Hitler was coming to prominence.* I thought of all the people who had opened all the doors for me on this journey, at this time of peril. How I'd moved from being the stranger who came to town to being an invited guest, from loneliness and dislocation to feeling connected and grounded through the people I had met along the way.

Back at the summer house, a robin had taken to breakfasting with me at the outside table, accepting crumbs of toast or cake that I placed in concentric circles closer and closer to my plate. One day, he followed me, flying into the house, and got caught against the windowpane. Both our hearts beat too fast as I flipped him out with a tea towel. This was not a good omen, I knew that much. In ancient lore, robins are capacious birds, they hold the souls of the dead.

A few days later I was sitting at the top of the cliffs at Es Caló Blanc, my favourite cove, cooling my heels after a long day's hiking and watching the water fish-sliding into rock pools when a naked woman with long black hair winding down her back strode down the narrow beach into the sea. She leaned backwards in the shallows to submerge herself, dark hair uncurling in the clear water, looking like something straight out of a myth or a painting. She scooped and swallowed eight handfuls of salt water in short succession and calmly walked out. It was the first time I'd ever seen anyone else down here, let alone swimming, let alone drinking seawater.

I turned to see that a tall man with white hair and glasses had materialised on the cliffs and was arranging red towels on the rocks. '*Hola,*' I called over, 'what's she doing?'

'Oh, Carmen follows the dolphin diet,' he said, as if that explained everything, as if that explained anything. He then proceeded to take all his clothes off.

Naked Andrew was almost seventy, an enthusiastic nudist, and British to the point of satire. He'd attended boarding school, his father called him 'Boy' even as a grown man, and he used to work in the City. In the first of several increasingly preposterous claims, he introduced himself as the 'King of Cala Fonts', the well-to-do harbour area beloved of expats in the town of Es Castell, and told me he often stopped at this particular cove for a quick swim on the drive to Carmen's house.

We never formally made plans to meet, at least at first, we'd just happen to both be in the cove around lunchtime, and slowly it became a routine and then an expectation, and then we would text if there was any delay. Usually, it was just Andrew, although sometimes Carmen joined us at the weekends. Occasionally he'd give me a lift if it was raining too hard to cycle.

I quickly learned that Andrew was nothing if not a man of rigid routine. First he sat down on 'his' shelf in our cove. This was a tiny sliver of slightly-less-uncomfortable rock. I was not permitted to sit here. I must instead sit on one of the uncomfortable rocks nearby. He would then arrange his three towels in a specified order that remained mysterious to me despite how much time we spent together, before liberally applying aloe vera all over his face. When I asked what this was for, he said it was like sunscreen and offered the same level of protection (it's not, it doesn't). Finally, he began combing the remainder of his white flowing hair carefully. Now he was ready for fully nude sunning, and as he undressed he took to sharing as many horror stories as he could think of with me.

'A six-foot big blue shark was sighted swimming casually close to shore in Cala Galdana, a popular tourist cove. It was starving and mean as hell. People took videos of it' – Andrew showed me a video on his phone – 'then it died because the island authorities dithered in guiding it back out to deeper water, I was rather cross about that.'

'It might be nice weather today but it certainly will not last. There will be very strong winds tomorrow, did you know that the tramontana wind is associated with an increase in suicide rates on the island?'

'A child's body was found in a suitcase, Menorca's biggest crime. The mystery has never been solved.' (I later found out this happened more than thirty years earlier – he had presented it as breaking news.)

'Someone went swimming, had his mouth open and there were jellyfish and one of them—'

At this last one I put my hands over my ears and screamed for him to stop. I wanted to sit in companionable silence, watch the colours of the sea and do my best to avoid getting an eyeful of his gently browning upturned scrotum, but Naked Andrew was never someone to let contemplative silence get in the way of good conversation.

Most days the sea here looked unreal, like it had been touched up and airbrushed, a pouting model in a glossy magazine. On sunny days it appeared enticingly tropical, like a melting summer cocktail, an illusion swiftly exploded when I lowered myself in gasping with the cold, scream-singing – 'Like a bloody banshee,' Andrew said.

Some days I missed my sea-swimming solitude but mostly I enjoyed his company. Andrew always got into the sea faster than me and taunted me for being a coward, a wimp, an inadequate Alpha Female as I shivered my way in, but I always stayed swimming for longer so it evened out. I tried sometimes to get here earlier to attempt to meditate but Andrew interrupted me yelling out an enthused hello as he bounded down the sheer stone steps towards me, chattering even though I was too far away to hear. The exuberance of the white-whipped water going up over the rocks and into the air felt like throwing confetti at a wedding you really believe in. I could feel it getting warmer as the days spun out, could stay in for longer, shook less when I got out.

'What a day to be alive!' I screamed at Andrew, our ritualised exchange in the water once my breathing had normalised.

'What a day to be alive!' he would scream back as I barrel-rolled over and over in the waves.

It's very easy to make up story between the gaps but the reality is never quite what I imagine, Andrew's story which seemed on the surface to be a comedy was in fact tragic. He had worked with his high powered stock-broking wife for years in Nottingham. They came to the island by chance in the eighties after a travel agent mis-sold them a holiday, fell in love with the place, and decided not to have kids so they could retire here as early as possible. One year before the retirement date they'd been working towards, his wife became very unwell. She asked him to take her to Menorca to die. As she was dying, she instructed Andrew to find a Spanish girlfriend, and a year after she died, he met Carmen, a Buddhist interior designer who, in Andrew's words, was 'a major conspiracy theorist'. Carmen's beliefs included but were not limited to the earth being flat and the moon landing being fake, and she had a keen interest in the nano technology of graphene for reasons she was not prepared to disclose. 'I'm desperately in love with Carmen, life is just so interesting with her,' Andrew said, and I heard the truth in it, the sweetness. He said the loneliness had gnawed at him like mice during the year he was mourning, he'd put on weight, he'd been drinking too much. 'You wouldn't understand,' he said, 'what it's like to be that lonely.' I knew something of it but kept my counsel. And made sure to relentlessly tease him about the mice of loneliness.

I wanted to capture this strange time, to photograph Andrew at the cove. I was trying to take his portrait in black-and-white, and art directed his nudity, suggesting a certain placement of the thighs and hands that left at least some things to the imagination. I clicked and tried different angles until finally he was there, on the screen. My camera captured a certain nobility, Naked Andrew staring out to sea, one foot upturned, his skin and the rocks seeming continuous. A shore creature.

'Not a bad body for a seventy-year-old, eh?'

'I don't know, Andrew, I haven't seen many naked seventy-year-old men, sadly for me. I don't have a benchmark.'

'Well, I think I look rather good,' he said, snatching at my phone like a toddler, squinting at himself against the sun. 'Pretty great,' he reassured himself, 'send me a copy, girl.'

'It seems so strange,' my father said when I told him the latest instalment in the Naked Andrew soap opera, 'you swimming and me sitting by Bertha.' He called the wood burner in the house Bertha, after a machine in a cartoon I'd liked as a child. I'd realise later how many names my father gave things and people. Everyone he liked best had a moniker, a nickname, a term of endearment, often combined with geolocation. My friend Katharine was never just Katharine to him, always 'Katharine The Horse' because he'd first encountered her playing the role of a horse in a play we were in at university, an equine performance he had much admired.

We didn't talk for long, he was feeling tired. 'I love you,' I said every time now when I called him and he said it back readily, he never used to. I guess it was one of the changes the cancer had wrought, more love, or at least more ability to say it easily, despite everything. When he said it, it made him feel closer and further away from me all at once.

One weekend, my circumnavigation almost complete, I detoured slightly off the *Camí* to Torre d'en Galmés, a prehistoric village built by the Talayotic people, the same ones who'd turned Cales Coves into a necropolis. They lived on the island in the Bronze Age and had a thing about T-shaped stones, spending a lot of their time creating these monumental structures, by stacking two colossal stones together – each one up to five metres high and weighing up to thirteen tonnes – without mortar using the 'Cyclopean technique' (the one-eyed monster again). Legends swirl that these were tables for giants, and although archaeologists have various theories about their function, the one I like best is that they represent doors to the world of the gods – closed doors that mere mortals cannot pass through, but through which the gods can enter our world if the correct rituals are held. The sun glittered in a corner of the temple ruins, I sat and thought about giants striding across this landscape and I watched the light play across the stones, and all at once I was undone in this silent, ancient holy place, built by ancestral powers to unknown gods. I hadn't seen my father for almost eight months.

What was I doing? What was the point of all this walking in a circle?

I turned back to the path remembering that old line from a poem I was taught at school:

I have promises to keep
And miles to go before I sleep.

I walked back slowly as the sun spun through the pine trees and the waters flashed electric blue.

It was only afterwards, once I'd completed the walk, I realised I'd substituted the *Camí* for the *Camino*. I thought about how much I'd walked in circles around all the most important things in my life, never quite making a decision. How much time I had wasted.

'It will only be months now,' said my mother. It was a top secret phone call, she had locked herself inside the car inside the garage so he wouldn't hear, but still she whispered it. 'Probably three to six months, we're hoping for six.'

I felt myself puff like a viper, outraged, how could he not have told me?

'He told you what he wanted to tell you,' she said, I heard the shrug in her voice, 'we have to respect his decisions.' My mother, a trained nurse, knew everything needed to be led by the patient. But the patient in this case was my father and she was supposed to be my mother. She abdicated that role when he was initially diagnosed, becoming again what she was first of all, his partner, his wife. Any space to mother a grown-up daughter had become compressed. This was common, I'd understood, from what some of my oldest friends in the Dead Dads Club told me when I consulted them. I still needed my mother but understood at the same time. Everything all at once, everything all mixed up.

'Should I come?'

She said to stay. He wanted privacy in the house. There wasn't much I'd be able to do, I'd need to quarantine elsewhere, I wouldn't be able to stay with them, and that felt pointless. 'I'll tell you when you need to come,' she said, 'I promise.'

'Privacy for what?' I asked.

'Well, darling, he vomits a lot.'

Months, I thought. Six.

Wood pigeons cooed from the trees, the sound of my childhood. I was homesick, I wanted everything to go back to normal.

I called my brother, also a doctor. He said it wasn't just chemo that made my father vomit. The actual cancer could make a person vomit too. He said my mother called him from the car a lot. He tried to talk to them both every day. In this way my brother was better than me.

He sent me a photograph of my father with Willow, my new baby niece. Theo, her brother, was out of shot. The baby was plump and rosy-cheeked as my father held her up and somehow the contrast between them made me see something I'd been avoiding. I had configured my senses, a language I heard but refused to understand, I'd changed my eyes so I didn't see the deterioration. You can't see if you won't look. I hadn't wanted to know how they were diminishing him, the inevitable faltering of the drugs. The same way I refused to hear the false note of optimism in his voice when he talked of this last roll of the dice, didn't want to hear that he didn't believe it, that he was putting it on for me, sugaring the pill, a more experimental protocol. I couldn't look at the photograph of him and the baby for long because it was there. It was there in the thinning of the cheeks, like his bone structure was changing. I wanted to see him as he was, not what he was becoming. There were things I couldn't avoid knowing. Something had changed in his voice. It was more effortful, more hesitant, his liquid fluency, the fluidity of the words was stilted, the same way that in the photographs with my niece, in his beautiful architectural face with those high cheekbones, there was a gauntness. I made my voice cheerier, warmer in compensation. I became more amusing, I thought about how to spin up stories for him, make him laugh, hear him smile. Listening to a smile I think is even nicer than seeing one. The audio of a smile is one of the loveliest things I can think of.

He was holding her up high. He was smiling and smiling. I think this is what people mean when they say things are always clearer when you look back.

I still can't look at this photograph.

I was talking about boring things with my father, about mortgages, asking his advice.

After I hung up I called Katharine.

'I think this was maybe the last time my dad will tell me what to do,' I said.

'I know,' she said.

'He doesn't have a five-year fix,' I said.

'That's a terrible joke,' she said.

I started to cry, big gulping sobs, looking up at the sky.

'I hate crying,' I said while I was crying, 'it's stupid.'

'I know,' she said.

Sometimes she knew exactly what to say.

Everything felt bad. I felt bad about not talking to my father more. When we spoke I felt bad then too, about talking about mundane things, pressure to be sparkling, amusing, to tap dance for him. I felt bad when I heard the new wavering in his voice, the tiredness. I felt like we should be having epic, sweeping conversations. We should be talking in poems, cadence and rhythm and nothing left unsaid but I was so tired, I wanted to sleep all the time. It was one of this island's enchantments, apparently. 'People here have the longest life expectancy in all of Spain,' Francesca told me, 'because people sleep so much on this island.' Sleeping is avoidance. But it's also preparation.

'He's sleeping a lot now,' said my mother. 'Sometimes he wakes up and says he doesn't know if he's been asleep or not. I feel so sorry for him.'

Hearing this broke something inside me. I thought about it all the time, about him sleeping all the time and waking up and not knowing if he'd been sleeping. The cold panted up from the floor in the unheated summer house from deep underground. The sky turned grey.

When will I stop believing in myths?

When will I stop making up stories about different endings?

Dusk fell blue and heavy, scented with the promise of spring as I walked between the white houses of St Lluís and down the lane towards the summer house carrying a bag of oranges to juice for breakfast tomorrow. The back of my hair was still sea-licked and wet from my swim, my legs were aching from the long hike that afternoon in a pleasant used-up kind of way. Everything felt easy as the sharp crescent of the moon slipped up the sky and the stars began to burst. A farm dog barked a warning at the night, my phone buzzed in my pocket.

'You have to come home.'

'What?' It was my brother and he had the pull of gravity in his voice.

'He's going downhill rapidly,' he sounded strange, 'just get home as fast as you can.'

I knew when my robin flew into the house. I knew then.

Chapter Ten

The Dawn of My Return

Oxfordshire, England

Gentle death will come to you,

far from the sea, of comfortable age,

your people flourishing. So it will be

The prophet Tiresias to Odysseus

'He's going downhill,' my mother says when I arrive.

She is a nurse. My brother is a doctor. My brother's fiancée is a doctor. My dad was a doctor before he became The Patient. My whole family speaks in clinical lexicon to each other.

'What does that mean?' I say.

'It means he's less steady on his feet. The stairs are a bit of a struggle. He can't speak on the phone really, not for long. He's thinking more slowly. The painkillers are making him sleepy and foggy. I just want to prepare you, darling, before you go in to see him.'

I am not prepared. He is a bird man in a hospital bed, mouth open, eyes shut, looking for all the world like a ghoulish Victorian illustration of death.

I remember when my cat was dying, she still wanted to be stroked and butted her head into my hand, but I could feel all her bones so I didn't like to touch her spine. I should have stroked her. She was a good cat. I should try and be a better person.

'He is in some discomfort. We are trying to get the pain under control. The inflammatory markers are high. We had a feel of his abdomen and there's no blockage,' my brother says.

He is talking to my father's doctor who has come to check on him.

'We are trying to control the controllables,' my brother says to me.

'End of life care was your father's favourite part of being a GP,' my mother says, 'he felt it was the most special time.'

He knew about end of life care. He knew what would happen to him. He knew. My throat fills.

'I think he's looking more comfortable now,' says my father's doctor.

He's in the foetal position, drawn up, curled. To me this does not look comfortable. There is conspiracy here: everyone telling each other what they need to hear.

'He's stoic,' says my mother and this part is true.

❄

It's a sunny morning. We take him in the wheelchair into the kitchen to sit in the sun. It takes three of us to transfer him, to lift him, pivot him, hold him up, position the chair behind him, sit him down again.

'Let's hold hands, Dad,' I say when we eventually get there.

'Are your hands sticky?' he says, 'because I do not want my hands to become sticky.'

It's the longest sentence he's spoken to me.

I rage at the nurse outside, at this waste of words, there are many more important things to say, surely?

'People who are dying narrow their locus of control to their immediate physical environment,' says the nurse, 'he wants his hands to remain un-sticky because he can't wash them himself,' and it's true, my father has always been fastidious, but why reserve words for this? When I want so badly to hear different words, other words. 'Every time you think about sticky hands in the future it'll remind you of your dad,' the nurse says. He explains that dying people tend to not speak to family, they have to save their energy for when the doctor or priest comes.

'I don't care,' I say to the nurse, 'he's being a dick.'

The nurse nods. He's the best nurse. My father worked with him for years and asked specifically for this man to be there, in the end, to take care of him. This nurse has visited every single day. This nurse has given me his phone number and said I can text or call at any time. But I don't want to call or text at any time. I want to scream and I can't leave the house and there's nowhere to scream. I feel hot.

'I used to scream in the car in the garage,' my mother says, 'where he couldn't hear me.'

I hold the phone to my father's ear as he sits in the wheelchair and his old crooked smile returns as he listens to our cousin John from Ireland, and he looks like a boy again.

'He can't talk,' I tell Irish John, 'but he's smiling.'

He's smiling.

'So, let me just explain how the hospital bed works, see this remote control?' The occupational nurse is one of the nicest people I have ever met. She's cheerful but not saccharine, not fake. These people who spend their lives so close to death fascinate me. I find them to be full of grace, they look after the threshold between the living and the dead, easing their path. I cannot understand how they can do this job. 'This is how the bars go up and down, see? Now you try.'

I click them up and down. A bed. A cot. Raise and lower. Safety. Imprisonment.

'We can't let him get up any more in the wheelchair to go to the loo, he's too unsteady,' my brother says, 'if he falls he'll break a hip and then he'll be taken into hospital and he'll die there. We need to minimise all risk. He wants to die at home.'

The occupational nurse nods. She pulls up the bars.

My body holds inside it a wince.

Later:

'Take this down,' says my father imperiously, meaning lower the bars so he can get out of bed. The old blue of his eyes is filmed with grey from the drugs.

Slowly, my father's hands reach towards the bars.

'It's okay,' I say, 'you have to stay in the bed, we can't get you out because it's too dangerous, it's okay.'

I keep saying that it's okay like an idiot. Of course it's not okay, he wants to get out.

His fish white hands reach slowly, he finds the bars, he holds on to them.

I uncurl his hands and hold them in mine.

Starveling hands.

So soft and the exact same size as my hands.

I'd pressed them together to check, one of his against one of mine. Fingertips to palm, mine a perfect replica.

'You have man's hands,' said my friend Pella, laughing, watching us do this over dinner, years before.

I don't care. I like having his hands.

My father has always been a deeply private man. My mother and my brother change him. I am not allowed in the room when this happens.

'He wouldn't like it,' my brother says.

'They've been so good,' my father tells me, one of the rare times he speaks. I repeat it to my mother who lights like the dawn sky.

'Did he really say that?'

Later:

We are changing the sheets. The nurse showed us how they are designed to slip so my father can be moved along the bed easily without anyone hurting their backs.

'Ready?' says my brother.

My mother and I nod, holding handfuls of sheet.

'On the count of three we lift and slide north,' says my brother, 'is that clear?'

My mother and I start laughing and can't stop. We let go of the sheet.

'What's so funny?'

'Slide north,' I gasp between giggles, 'obviously we just pull him up the bed.'

'Look, if I'm in charge of this team—' starts my brother.

'You're not in charge of anyone,' I say. My brother rolls his eyes.

Later:

'Listen, he just feels a huge amount of responsibility as a doctor,' says my mother. 'It's hard for him, he's stressed.'

And then I feel sorry for my little brother and I feel lucky he's a doctor, which he's always acted superior about, but when he walks into the room I still say, 'Um, sorry, shall we go north?' and my mother snorts and he glares at me.

※

'When *will* Grandad die?' Theo asks. He is leaning over the hospital bed, playing across the bars.

'When he's ready,' my brother says.

A perfect answer.

Theo holds my father's hand, he doesn't seem bothered by how different he looks, or that he's just lying there with his eyes shut. He accepts him like this, shows him a Lego car he's built.

'Look, it has tyres on the roof!'

He can't open his eyes.

'Tyres on the roof is an amazing idea,' I say, speaking for my father.

Later:

Theo is holding my hand.

I feel something moving across my palm.

'What are you doing?'

'Stroking you,' he's moving his thumb across my hand over and over.

I hug him. He wriggles. He runs.

※

'He would love this,' my mother says, 'all of us in the house together again, he wants to stay with us, I think he's enjoying it. Like Christmas.'

It's not like Christmas.

❋

My brother brings my baby niece into the room. My father has only met her once because of the pandemic. She's sleeping. He hasn't opened his eyes for days but when he hears her name he opens his eyes.

She opens her eyes.

They look at each other for a long time.

They gaze.

Something happens to the light in the room.

❋

This evening, in his wheelchair, he hugs and hugs my mother, on her knees beside him. Stroking her hair. He won't let go.

❋

Slowly everything is taken from him. The cancer drugs are stopped. Sips turn to straws turn to syringes of water that we carefully squirt into his mouth. His swallow migrates. Now we dip pink medical lollipop-sponges in ice water and move them like dentists around his mouth. 'Mouth care is really important,' says my brother, 'we don't want it to get sore from being open all the time.'

❋

He has drawn his legs up into a foetal position. He is taking up less and less room in the bed. Sometimes his legs shake. I worry it is pain and he can't speak to tell us so I hold his legs and make a support from yoga bolsters, make them into a triangle. Slowly they relax into my hands, slowly the shaking stops. His legs have become so thin. Most of him is bird now.

❄

It's been a week, it's been longer than a week, and I ask everyone who comes, priests, nurses, palliative care specialists, the GP, when, when will he die?

'Probably not long now, but it's impossible to predict,' a Greek chorus, the low hum of respectful church voices. I want to force them at gunpoint to give me a proper answer at a normal fucking volume.

'Your dad must have lion's blood or dragon's blood or something,' says my favourite nurse, 'he's so strong.'

I tell Theo that he has lion's blood and dragon's blood inside him. Theo roars. I roar back.

'Say goodnight to Daddy,' my mother says, every night, the implication is he may not be alive in the morning. This is exhausting.

One of the nurses tells me 'most people cross over at four in the morning'. She sits calmly, knitting, watching, ready to soothe. 'They get agitated at night, they want to get out of bed, it's like they want to get away,' she says. No shit.

❄

We are alone. I pull his arm over me and lie there, against the uncomfortable bars at the side of the hospital bed. An arranged hug.

✳

There is a vase of bluebells in the room. There are bluebells in the woods we used to walk in. There's a savage beauty to these days. It's a leaping, beautiful spring. Outside there are bluebells.

✳

'Can you give me away?' says Sarah, my brother's fiancée, bursting into my father's study upstairs where I am hiding/working.

'What?'

'We're getting married! Now!' And she's smiling this big, huge smile. She takes my hand and pulls me.

There's a priest downstairs that no one has ever met before, I don't catch his name. I knew he was arriving at the house to give Last Rites and pay his respects but something must have happened.

'What's going on?' I say.

'Darling, can you hold my phone, hang on, how do I get Sarah's mum on video?' says my mother. 'Oh, is it this button? Can you hear me?'

'I can hear you!' says Sarah's mother from Trinidad. 'Hi, everyone!'

'Look, it's not official,' says the priest, 'but at least your father will be there. It won't be legally binding, I can only do a blessing, I can't get in trouble with the archbishop for this sort of thing again,' then he winks at my brother and my brother grins and then looks serious and nervous.

My mother starts to cry. 'Isn't this just wonderful?' she says.

I don't know what to say.

'Do you, Douglas, take this woman—' says the priest.

'Duncan,' says my brother.

'Do you, *Duncan*, take this woman Sarah to be your lawfully wedded wife?' the priest intones. He's standing on one side of my father's actual deathbed, my brother and Sarah are standing together on the other side.

My father is in his usual position: silent, mouth open, eyes shut.

My arm aches from holding out the phone at the right angle so Sarah's mother can see. They were supposed to be married in Trinidad in the spring when the pandemic first unfurled its claws.

The priest proceeds through the entire marriage ceremony. It seems like it's not just a blessing, it seems like my brother is possibly now married.

'Amen,' says the priest.

'Amen,' says my father in a tiny voice, and everyone twists simultaneously like at a tennis match: he hasn't spoken for days. 'Open some champagne!' says my father in his new tiny voice that's really just a whisper.

'Did you hear that?' my brother says. 'He said to open some champagne! Sarah, did you hear that?'

My father is not fully sedated by the drugs, despite every appearance to the contrary, he's actually here, he's with us, he's *here*.

Everyone is laughing, champagne pops. My mother is exultant. My brother's eyes have gone bright pink like one of those white rabbits. He is hugging Sarah, my mother is speaking on the phone to Sarah's mother, the priest is holding my father's hand. I'm breathing fast, hard and staccato but the oxygen isn't working properly, I have to go outside into the cold of the night air to get it together.

I think I'm having a panic attack. Slowly my breathing shakes down to normal again.

Later:

'There's been a deathbed wedding,' I say to Rachel on the phone.

'What?' she says. 'Are you serious?'

'Just when you thought it couldn't get any more melodramatic,' I start laughing, 'it was kind of amazing,' I say.

'His organs are starting to fail now, you can see that the liver is getting too big for the liver capsule. If he wasn't on these painkillers he'd be in terrible, agonising pain,' my medical mother says. Precision missiles in clinical language.

He can't speak. I never realised they'd take that away from him, the drugs, I had always thought we'd be able to talk. It is in conversation that my father is best. I had not anticipated that I would be gagged, he would be drugged, speech effortful for both of us. Eventually I stop trying to say bright and breezy things. I start to sit. That's what vigil means, to keep watch where worlds collide. The known world, the world of the living and the world of the gods, where myth and stories and babies come from. He's sliding there, slowly. Nothing can stop him except himself, and he doesn't want to go, *not yet, not yet,* he's saying, I think.

✳

I'm trying not to cry, to keep a stiff upper lip. My brother openly weeps in front of my father. This surprises me.

'He'd have hated this show of emotion,' I say to Katharine on the phone, 'he hated anyone crying.'

My mother told me she pre-secured a waiver, before he got this ill. 'I told him he has to let me cry,' she says. When they moved the bed downstairs my father asked my mother to keep the light on all night and not to leave him. She promised. This is their deal, but she can only go part of the way with him. She sleeps next to the hospital bed every night. 'I'm here darling,' she says loudly whenever she enters the room, everyone is speaking more loudly now, my father had been going a little deaf, even before all this. 'You're getting ready for your journey, aren't you, darling?' she says, stroking his hair, his face. 'You can leave whenever you're ready,' she says, 'I'll be okay, darling.' The nurse has said it's important to give the dying permission to leave.

'You can cry if you want to. He's not what he was,' says Katharine, 'underneath it all he's a deeply feeling man.'

'I don't want him to change. I want him to be exactly as he was, or dead,' I say.

I will not cry in front of him.

Not as he is: open-mouthed, cling-film eyes, swimming down somewhere in the depths, not speaking, under cover of drugs, but back the way he was, should be: funny, animated in conversation, walking next to me in the woods, looking for strangers to talk to, amusing them, interrogating them, alert for fun.

He is distilling into himself, getting lighter every day. He's evaporating.

✳

It has been days without count. This liminal space, this hanging, this suspended solution, chalky-white in a test tube held to the light, is too hard. Everything hurts in my throat. Suffocated howls and fish-bone trapped words. I'm supposed to be good with words, to be able to string them, and I can't figure it out, the Last Words, what to say to him.

I interrogate my brother, the weight of it heavy on my neck. 'What do you say to him?'

'It's private, I'm not telling you.' He's in there for hours alone with him, whispering to him. What is he saying?

'What should I say?' I ask my mother.

'Say whatever you like,' she says, but I want to be told, exactly.

You're the most ungrateful person in the world.

Remembering that big argument makes me hot. I'm going to get it wrong. It feels pressured, squeezed, last chance. It feels like cowboy saloon doors swinging. I look it up. There is an algorithmically recommended answer. I try it out loud and it sounds thickly fake.

I can't find words.

He's deep-sea diving. He's moving between worlds, exploring and pulling back, held by my mother's grief. He's getting ready to depart for the world of the immortals.

✳

Morphine has stolen my father's wit, his humour, his voice. Now he swims slowly, breathes rhythmically. My mother has started speaking to him and for him, the way you do for a pre-verbal child.

※

Sharp blue eyes gone grey.

I can't bear this agonised waiting. No one is sleeping. The house is a cage. I long to swim, to slide into the water, to have something bear my weight, take his weight.

※

The living translate the dying. When they will not talk any more, self-anointed spokespeople divine needs, interpret emotions, speak for them, and in this second-hand way they say they love you, they're glad you're home even if they cannot speak it, even if it took you too long.

There's a statistic, I can't remember the details, anyway, something about how people slip away when their loved ones nip out to grab food or go to the bathroom. That's when many people choose to die. In the space between, when they're not held down by love, I guess. When it's lighter and easier to slide into the water.

※

I want him to hurry up and die and release us all. I want him to never die. You wouldn't put a dog through this, I think. I don't say this to my mother or my brother.

⁂

I am reading out loud to him, all the long, funny emails he sent from his holidays. I am reading him back to himself, and we travel from the Annapurna mountains in Nepal to Kerala in South India, from Lake Geneva to a rainstorm in Italy, along an ancient pilgrimage route in Spain and into the streets of Cuba. One last grand voyage to all the beauties of the world.

⁂

The doorbell rings. On the doorstep: a bunch of bright red rhubarb tied with string, and some flowers. 'I thought you might like these – from our garden,' says the note, 'we're thinking of you,' says the note, 'please tell us if there's anything we can do,' it says.

But there's nothing you can do.

My brother makes rhubarb crumble. We eat like feral, starving animals. My father has not eaten for nine days. I am worried he's hungry and not able to tell us. The nurse says this is not the case but I'm not sure I believe him.

⁂

There are other things that happen too but I can't write them. There is horror, charred remains. Black blank blur goes my mind. I go upstairs to work in my father's study because I'm freelance and I'm paid by the day. Also, if I'm honest, because I want to escape.

I work in the blank. Later my boss will ask me about a meeting. I'll have no recall. 'But you presented, you answered all the questions,' he'll say.

'It's all Rohypnol,' I'll tell him.

Black blank blur, my mind, protecting me. I should not be working but what else is there I can do? I lie on the carpet and look up at the ceiling, I get up and look through his bookshelves, he's kept a note from teenage me, he's framed it:

'I'm recording *Shallow Grave*, don't turn this off or you'll end up in one.'

✳

When Odysseus finally makes it home he sees his elderly father in the orchard 'worn by age', and is so 'heart-wrenched' to see him like this that he has to stop by a pear tree to weep. Then he lies to his dad, who doesn't recognise him, pretending to be a friend of his long-lost son. When he reveals the truth the old boy faints, overwhelmed by emotion. Fuck Odysseus.

✳

His whole body has become a heart, all of it seems to beat. His hairline changes, his nose thins, becomes more aquiline. He looks noble. Is suffering noble? I don't think so. I think of Jesus up on his crucifix, holy, writhing, the agonies of death. At least he knew exactly where he was going.

❄

Theo's syrupy little body blurs and shifts hundreds of times a day as he slips between realms, real and imagined, the same way my father slips between this world and the next. He's a lemur, a snapping turtle, a rainbow tiger, then a boy again.

❄

'We simply ADORE your dad. Always have. Always will', texts my cousin. I read this message over and over. I like the word adore, I like the capital letters she's used, I like this cousin very much, and I like that my father means something to her.

❄

'I'm about to post your great-grandmother's rosary to you. When you feel the beads between your fingers you will know that your grandmother and her mother prayed these beads to Our Lady. We hope you are comforted by this,' says someone I've never even met from Ireland.

When the rosary arrives the stamps are pictures of *Father Ted*, a show my father loved. These small details, this care. I wrap the beads around his hands, I don't know how to pray a rosary, I think it's mostly Hail Marys.

✳

'Please tell Paul we are praying to St Martin to intercede with the Almighty on his behalf,' says my father's friend.

✳

I want the sea and shore and sky back.

✳

'Dad said "I love you" to me this morning,' I say to my brother, 'yet more evidence I am the favourite one.'

'Yeah. Keep telling yourself that,' my brother says. He looks like my father. As he passes he puts his hand on my shoulder, he squeezes it.

'You're my favourite,' I say to Theo.

'No, but you're my favourite,' Theo says, starting a game.

✳

My mother is curled around her darling darling darling.

✳

I have left the house for the first time in ten days.

15:23.

The phone rings once.

'Laura?' says my brother.

My brilliant brother.

※

Doctor Paul Coffey died today at 15:20 at home with his family beside him.

※

(I wasn't there.)

※

He is/was my father.

Chapter Eleven

Under Snow

Oxfordshire and London, England

Grief wrapped around her, eating at her heart

In *The Odyssey* the gods are immoral immortals, ambivalent, petty and rude. Athena, Odysseus's champion, intervenes right at the end of the story to make peace in the chaos she has authored. A sleight of hand, some fake news of its day, but everything gets resolved. That's how endings should work.

This was a godless time. I lay in my childhood bed, sleep blown apart, listening to my mother cry. Before this, I had gone with her to visit the freshly dug grave so she could talk to it: 'Hello darling, I hope you are free, I hope your pain has gone now, and the nausea.'

The world unlocked, spinning up again after pandemic restrictions lifted, and I was under snow. I'd stayed free in lockdown, now I was trapped in the house I'd grown up in, had travelled home to be with my father when he was dying, only to miss the most important bit. It was ironic. It should have been funny, but nothing felt funny any more.

In the church my mother flinched when I tried to put my arm around her. I was worried people in the pews behind might think it odd, cruel, me not touching her. Wicked, heartless, broken daughter. I tried again, and again she went rigid, and I realised she was holding herself together, bone and sinew and ligaments. My touch risked piercing her composure, she needed to endure this new aloneness alone. She was being brave.

'I wish he'd dropped dead.'

I was not allowed to say this. It was not a nice thing to say. The line was censored by my brother. What I meant was I would have spared him the foreshadowing, had him struck by lightning instead of this slow fading, chosen sudden death instead of all the weighing and measuring of treatment options that held the line, until they all failed one by one, to be replaced by poison then opiates. What I meant was that I'd been sharply jealous of a friend who lost her grandfather suddenly in the pandemic, that I'd been envious, even as I saw how shocked she was. I sat in the heavy church on the scented dark pews like an animal and I thought about saying it anyway, when I stood up to speak, but ended up not saying the line, and felt I betrayed myself, had been betrayed. Grief incompleted, suspended, hibernates through snow.

There are tiny weird things we do to make ourselves feel safe. My brother, when he was very small and very blonde and beautiful, had a large collection of pebbles he'd curated from various walks, so many that they formed a sort of art installation in his bedroom. Before he left the room, the house, he had to touch them all in a certain order. It was a form of magical thinking, a ritual, and after my father died, I watched my mother doing the same thing. Tapping a particular light switch a set number of times before flicking it off.

Back in London, I was absent, did things mechanically, a heavy, clockwork girl. I landed badly on my lockdown trampoline, heard a bright snap, cycled to the hospital using the other leg. My ankle was broken. I use exercise to lift myself away from things, to regulate, feel better, it was a 'coping mechanism' the doctor said, and now it would be impossible. From constant motion I was forced to slow, to be still, to wait, for eight to twelve weeks. I sucked the pain through me, its sharpness gave me edges. Perhaps I'd wanted to hurt myself. It would be too clumsy to say I was losing my footing in the world, too obvious to interpret this as an external manifestation of something deep and broken and painful inside me, too banal to observe I was no longer grounded.

I walked around in the boot the doctor gave me but it did not immobilise the bones properly, didn't hold me tight enough. The pain scratched through. My brother came with a better boot and strapped me into the Velcro like a child.

Months slipped, the sky turned grey and colourless as summer faded in from spring and I felt how thin and slender everything was. I had become an island, remote, unreachable, covered in sea fog.

'I know why you're sad, Daddy,' Theo said to my brother, 'you miss Grandad, you want to go to heaven and find him.'
I missed Theo.

'Trust your sense of humour will come back,' an old boyfriend said.
'Will it?'
'I promise.'
'When?'
It didn't feel like anything would ever change. I limped, dragging the boot.

I went swimming, up and down, twisted and turned in artificially blue chlorinated water contained inside overheated pools instead of the cold, expansive sea. I kept kicking my ankle even though it hurt. A robot self inside a real girl, on automatic, but some part of me knew how to get stronger.

Sometimes I thought about who I'd trade for him. Who I wish had died instead. If I could have the choice. If I could choose.

I still wanted my wedding speech, even though there was no wedding.

'Darling, he couldn't write it for you, he couldn't write or speak much in the last weeks,' my mother said.

'I asked years before that,' I said, throat collapsing.

She, official spokesman and defender-to-the-hilt of the canonised memory of my late father, did not understand why I was so upset. There were always gaps in understanding between us. I am more like my father is. Was. We understood each other better.

'He spent longer on the surgery charity than my fake wedding,' I said to Pella, hearing the absurdity as I said it and she explained it, kindly, quietly, 'Maybe it was too sad for him, maybe he just couldn't face it.'

It was too sad for him.

It was too sad for me.

Part of me knew that I wasn't really angry about the speech. I was angry at him. For disappearing

I lay in the snow, holding on to my shard, is/was.

I was terrified of what I read about 'unresolved grief'. What could possibly resolve it? I visited his grave only once. He wasn't there.

I cycled to Katharine's flat wearing the boot even though it was obviously very stupid. I needed my bicycle back, needed to be on the move more than I feared hurting myself again. I knew I was bad company, knew I was holding the shape of myself but none of the content. Katharine lit a yellow candle at her table and started addressing it as CandleDaddy. It was weird and perfect.

'Salutations, Paul Coffey,' she said, 'how the devil are you?'

We spoke to CandleDaddy and light flickered around the room. She made me eat properly, burned sage and cleansed me, its acrid smell and grey smoke filling the air until she started to worry about her fire alarm going off. I cycled home through the green black park. Starlight couldn't reach past the light pollution but the orange moon hung heavy in the sky.

I screamed loudly, once, when I got home, and denied it when a concerned neighbour knocked on my door to ask if I'd heard someone in the building screaming?

'No,' I said, flatly.

'I'm really worried. It was blood-curdling. You sure you didn't hear anything?'

'The soundproofing is weird here,' I said, shrugging.

'I hope they're okay,' he said, looking at me oddly.

I stared at him until he left.

There are no safe places to scream in a city.

I dropped a wine glass on my kitchen floor and it shattered into a million tiny shards, skittering everywhere. I shut the kitchen door, walked out of the flat, got onto my bicycle and rode away. When I came back the floor was still covered in glass. I crunched across it in my boot to get a glass of water. Went to bed.

My brain was strange. I read that cognitive function declines for people grieving. What was the difference between grief and mourning? Moments came back: his legs trembling, a neighbour asking how I was and me responding that I wouldn't put a dog through that, and her physically stepping back away from me, my words had snarl, had violence in them. Bluebells in the woods.

My friend Ros, who was part of the Dead Dads Club, told me to remember grief is physical, gets into your body, makes you tired. 'You'll think you're thinking straight,' she said, 'but you won't be.' I was trying not to think at all.

In *The Odyssey*, Helen of Troy spikes the wine at dinner with a drug that takes away the capacity to feel grief, anger, pain. I needed Helen's drugs.

I wanted to melt into the sea. I wanted to dissolve into salt and atoms. Francesca said, 'Just get on a plane, come to Menorca, I can pick you up in a wheelchair,' but the snow was too deep and I couldn't move.

'I wish I had some words of comfort to offer you,' my father once told me on a green spring day as we walked together through my favourite wood, me upset about life which was at the time feeling abortive, about the future which had started to feel like it was closing down. He was pretending I wasn't crying and then I was shouting at him for trying to make my tears invisible. His default with all emotions was to ignore them, pretend they weren't happening, not to feel but instead to think, I wish I had some words of comfort to offer you. A strangely formal thing to say, but then he did have a formality to him. Perhaps that's the reason I can't seem to write 'dad', I have to say my father.

The thing I miss most is our conversation. I would have better last words now. I'd be able to find exactly the right ones for love. For imperfection.

Chapter Twelve

Poetry of *The Odyssey*

Returning to the islands

Dawn on her golden throne began to shine

Poems repeat. People do too. Eventually my ankle healed. Eventually I moved.

In the car ride down from Palermo to Trapani to catch the ferry I was seized by a thought: what if it didn't work this time? It clutched me by the stomach – if my islands couldn't fix me I wasn't sure what could. Under usual circumstances I never want to go back, to repeat. I prefer to travel on, find new places to explore. The pandemic was supposedly over. I wasn't following Odysseus any more – a girl was lost at sea after a storm but what if I couldn't find her, even here? I felt carsick and hot, lay down across the back seat and closed my eyes. The dark Sicilian night spun beneath the tyres, warm and endless.

If you can't find a person in the world you can find a landscape. I wanted to be held by space this time instead of being in motion, but when I arrived the island was more strange than it was familiar. Known and unknown all at the same time. It had the same contours but within them everything had changed. It was an odd, dislocating feeling, like returning to New York City only to find the restaurants and shops I had loved had shifted or closed, the city had moved on. Nothing stays the same forever except within the embellishments of imagination.

In Favignana everything was open and easy, the bars and restaurants had tables on the terraces full of tourists, straw baskets outside shop fronts swung in the wind, in Caffè Aegusa on the main square Italians guzzled *brioche con gelato* for breakfast, the beaches were dizzy with parasols and sun-smoked bodies and colourful stripy towels and orange deckchairs facing the sea. The whole place felt light and summery, it was hot even though it was nearly autumn, and in contrast I'd turned heavy, half-ghost, haunting the old places looking for resolution. The water blazed bright with summer blues and wasn't cold enough to shock me, everything felt more normalised. I missed the empty strangeness, needed to feel the cold flooding through me, wanted the rush of it, to feel embodied again, not just a hot mind whirring in my heavy head. Now that everything was normal again nothing was normal again. Naked Andrew texted that he'd been in hospital, they were doing exploratory tests. I couldn't bear anyone else near me to be sick, to have cancer.

I should have known that I couldn't repeat myself, could never travel backwards. Mythical islands by their nature are especially elusive. Just when you think you have them mapped, they shift and change. I felt out of time, out of place, disjointed.

There's a lot of repetition in *The Odyssey*. Homer uses a formulaic kind of language, describing things in a certain way, and these phrases recur, looping through the poem. The sea, for example, is always 'wine-dark' and 'moon pulled', Athena is 'bright eyed', Dawn is 'newborn' and 'rosy'. Emily Wilson notes that repetition was important in oral traditions because it gives 'a listener an anchor in a quick-moving story'. However, now we consume poetry by reading instead of listening and Emily acknowledges that all this deliberate repetition gets quite boring. So she riffs, creating jazz translations and remixes, playing around with what's possible inside the constraints of particular turns of phrase. In Emily's translation, Dawn becomes whimsical. She changes every time she relights the sky, ascending in her 'golden throne'. 'Soon Dawn appeared and touched the sky with roses', or 'when early Dawn shone forth', or 'Dawn on her golden throne began to shine', or 'Dawn who dances in meadows with the beams of Helius', although there remain disturbing descriptions of Dawn's 'rosy fingers' and, particularly weird, 'rosy fingered Dawn', which recurs more times than I'd like.

I had never considered translation to be a creative act before, not that I'd really thought particularly deeply about it, but as I read the poem again and noticed this wordplay I saw that Emily was exposing her power, showing me how a translator can shade a text as she skates across one language, sliding it into another. A translator chooses what to emphasise, what to tweeze, how colloquial, loose and baggy the words can go, or conversely how much they need to be constrained, buttoned into formality. It's Emily who is determining texture and cadence – translation is far more than a straightforward conversion from one thing into another. She says there's 'no such thing as a translation that provides anything like a transparent window through which a reader can see the original' and reading her version I could see how she had fun, fencing with words and meter, and in this latitude, her mastery was clear, and transmitted something to me. I started thinking more about translation and about being translated. It is a fundamentally interpretative act, to provide a reading of the story, and then of course we add our own interpretation on top of that. Layers on layers. It makes sense that Penelope is constantly weaving and unweaving because that's how story works. There is no definitive translation, no single way of rendering text, of receiving it. There will always be gaps in the meanings between words, in the truth of things. There's no absolute way to prevent being misunderstood, of mitigating the risk of a bad translation.

I needed seawater to soothe the last months out from me, to go numb, dissolve myself in salt, to swim, to rehabilitate my ankle, feel the ground steady beneath me again. Every day at twilight I slipped into the sunset and swam, the light was pink and the sea glowed. 'Opacarophile' is a combination of Latin and Greek words meaning sunset chasers. Literally translated it means 'lover of dusk', imaginatively translated it contains something vampiric in it, I think. In London I rarely noticed a sunrise or a sunset. I was detached from the moon cycles and the night skies, from the sea and its rhythms, never knowing the wind speed or the direction it was blowing from. Back on the island, I got up very early each day to see the sunrise. Watched as pink licked across the ice-cream sky and just as quickly fell out of it. You have to pay attention to catch it. You have to look up to see Dawn, see how she moves across the sky, holding flowers in her arms.

Odysseus repeated part of his journey, like me he also went back, only he didn't mean to. They were within sight of home when the crew opened up that bag of winds which blew the ship all the way back, right across the sea, to where they started. When Odysseus washed up for a second time on his shore, exasperated Aeolus, ruler of the winds, was slightly less welcoming.

Get out!
You nasty creature, leave my island! Now!…
You godforsaken thing, how dare you come here?

Theo loves repetition. He asks for the same stories over and over. In children's books you can always go back to the start. The day after the funeral, we had been walking together in the green woods picking up sticks and dipping them in puddle water and river water. Double protection against monsters.

'What bit did you like? The bit where we played songs, or when we told stories about Grandad?'

'I liked the part when we planted Grandad.'

He meant the burial, he had watched the coffin being lowered into the ground on ropes and covered over with earth and grass.

Planted. The most beautiful translation. Years after this, someone I work with will tell me her baby has died and how she's struggling most with having to put him into the earth. '*You planted him,*' I will say, and Theo's words will unlock something for her too. Language does matter. Events can be interpreted many ways, and there are always words of comfort if you find the right translator.

Why had I come back to this island? I was trying so hard to look at things differently, or more accurately, to find a new way of seeing. Or maybe it was far more basic than that, I wanted to go backwards because the future felt too broken.

———

It was December in Menorca again, almost Christmas again, and the cold skies were blue bright. Each morning I took a coffee to the roof terrace, sat in the blues in my coat and scarf and watched the weathervane spin. I read a poem and cried, compressed emotions, folded in like origami inside the poem, inside me. Crying and reading poetry. I know how that sounds, but at the funeral someone had told me we're each given a quota of tears that have to be cried, and you just can't do anything about it. Remembering this made me feel better as tears slid off my jaw onto my neck. I wiped at them impatiently.

I don't know precisely what my father believed about the Catholic version of the afterlife. He would never tell me, despite me asking in different ways. I had even strong-armed his priest in the vestry after the funeral to interrogate him but he too refused to answer anything. Confessional confidentiality applied, it seemed, beyond the grave, beyond irritating. I wanted him to tell my father back to me, to intermediate, to interpret his faith in a way I could understand. I'm not sure what I believe either, but there's something in the idea of liminal spaces, corridors, and thresholds that demarcate between-spaces, transience, passage and crossing places. Of keeping vigil, watching over the dying. I had seen the guardianship of the palliative care team, how they held these spaces with quiet grace, opening doors between worlds.

I walked back into the village of St Lluís with its small white houses, down streets I'd walked so many times before. In the way of islands, I bumped straight into Javier, the ornithologist, who told me he was going bird ringing. The way he said it sounded like bells but I knew he meant the science of catching birds and fitting them with rings to understand their migration patterns and better inform conservation efforts.

'Maybe I could come?' I blurted out.

Javier looked at me, head cocked, something of the bird in him, and smiled. 'I'll look to the weather for next week and tell you which day I go.'

I held it close to me, this vague, weather-dependent plan. The future calling instead of the exhausting pull of the past. I waited for Javier's text, checking my phone with the obsessiveness of new lovers. When it finally pinged with instructions I was too excited to sleep. I had to be ready very early in the morning because the nets must be set up in the dark, before the birds woke. Waiting outside in the December dark for Javier's headlights, blurry-eyed, watching as my breath smoked through the air, felt like a beginning, a promise of something new.

In the cold darkness lit green by our head torches, Javier and I set up the nets around the site, on a dairy farm, walking through fields of thistles and nettles. I'd lost feeling in my fingers, my feet were wet from the long grass, and I kept stumbling over unseen things, getting stung and pricked, while Javier, green eyes glowing in the blackness, was sure-footed. We worked together in the dark silence unfurling the nets. When I touched them, they felt sticky, clinging to my finger pads. Javier said they were Japanese, apparently Spanish nets were nothing like as good. When we had finished, there were long lateral nets, slightly higher and longer versions of the type strung up on a lazy summer's day to play badminton barefoot in the garden. They had to be placed in the exact same location every single time to ensure continuity. This was science, after all. I asked why the birds didn't just fly upwards, avoiding the nets. 'But they don't see them,' Javier said, slowly, clearly wondering at the depths of my stupidity. From where we were putting the nets it seemed birds fly much closer to the ground than I'd thought. After a couple of hours all the fields were set up and we waited outside the farmhouse for the sun to come up, for the birds to start to fly.

It wasn't a spectacular sunrise, just a slow egg yolk orange. Pricked into an animal alertness in the predawn darkness I hopped from foot to foot in the cold as the sky pressed itself against dark trees across the fields, slowly outlining them. My legs nettle-stung, my feet soaking wet, my arms scratched, with tender places beginning to bruise from where I'd banged them and I was happy, stamping my feet, trying to get warm, waiting.

The farmer's wife took pity, brought us cups of scalding coffee and biscuits in a red tin. I curled my hands around the cup, my fingers warmed up enough for me to pull off my soaked shoes and socks, preferring being cold to being wet. I itched at my legs and knew I'd crossed a line. Going bird ringing was definitely several levels up in the bird-nerd game. A few stings were a small price to pay.

At this site, the nets had to be hung out three times in winter and seven times throughout the summer. It took one full day to set everything up, put the poles up ready, and a second day to open the nets, to catch and count the birds and report the findings. Javier looked after several sites across the island and normally didn't have anyone to help him.

'Is it paid?'

'Enough to replace the nets when they break.' He held up his hand to stop me asking questions. 'Hear that?'

Something called across the long darkness, low and insistent.

'A partridge,' said Javier, delighted, as if he hadn't heard this a billion times before.

We listened into the silence again. Another cry, this time more of a squeaky wail, cut through the morning.

'That's a stone curlew, a wader, he hunts at night. He is now looking for a place to spend the day, to relax.'

'To relax?' I checked that this was the bird's entire plan for the whole day.

'Yes, to relax.'

I loved how Javier translated the sounds of the night, matched calls to birds. A decoding. Like spinning stars into astrology. I flexed my numb feet and held my coffee mug against my stomach. I was wearing multiple layers as instructed, but Menorca's damp winter cold penetrated regardless.

As the sun rose higher, Javier became increasingly serious. He briefed me on our strict schedule: we must check all the nets every single hour. 'The birds must not be left any longer than that,' he said sternly, as if I was about to propose leaving them for long periods. 'The first priority, number one, is the birds' well-being.'

I nodded solemnly. We waited for more light.

Dawn caught in the billows of the nets, turning them golden, as Javier set up our temporary desk on a table in front of the milking barn. Seven different sizes of bird rings, threaded around large hooping coils, clinked as he put them down next to a knife-sharpened pencil. Three books on birds stacked in height order, including the authoritative *Collins Bird Guide*. Two different sizes of fine pliers, the sort that jewellers have, a metal ruler, a small set of digital scales, two plastic cups: a blue one and a much smaller white one. A black clipboard holding a stack of papers pre-ruled into thin columns, ready to be filled in.

Yellow-throated screaming pierced the morning. It sounded like a person, like a human baby, nothing at all like a bird. Wings beat against the net, feet clawed, tangling, the brown bird became increasingly frenetic as we walked nearer. It hurled insults at us, high-pitched swearing, and when its cursing had no effect on our approach, changed tack and started crying pitifully instead. Crying as if we were murdering its chicks and making it watch, crying as if we were smashing up its eggs in front of it, scrambling them for breakfast and licking our chops. 'They're always like that.' Javier shrugged. The man was lake calm.

It was a song thrush, fairly big and heavy, about the same size as a blackbird. When I'd seen them in the wild I hadn't thought they looked particularly special – their wings are a dullish brown – but up close I could see a fat white speckled stomach, each splash shaped like a teardrop, beautiful in the morning light, and the bright neon yellow of the inside of its beak as it opened to scream. Javier gently untangled it from the net but I had to turn away. It was like watching that part in a horror film when the monster is coming closer and closer, and the heroine is trying to get away but keeps fumbling with the car keys. I had that same light-headed screaming-accelerated feeling. The bird's panic had got inside me. I wanted Javier to go faster, release it quicker, but he remained calm and slow and methodological, the scientist, always. This bird didn't know it, but it was in expert hands.

Seeing my distress, Javier turned philosophical. 'The stress is worth it so we can get the information to protect them and their habitats.' I somehow hadn't considered this, that there would be struggle, terror, screaming. What was I thinking? That we'd prance around with butterfly nets catching pretty birdies that wouldn't mind? Trapped in flight by something invisible, I'd scream too. 'They don't like it,' said Javier, 'how would you feel if someone caught you and put you in a bag and put a bracelet on you?'

I thought of being tangled up in a net. I thought about my head being put in a bag.

I held open a soft cotton bag with purple stains from frightened previous occupants who had literally lost their shit, and Javier put the song thrush in, head down, still screaming. It screamed and screamed and struggled inside the bag, would not stop moving and screaming. I admired this rage, knew it well. Javier and I moved clockwise around the nets, untangling birds. A tiny, dignified robin, silent, calm, less panic-tangled and so easier to release, went into a separate bag. My job was to open the bags for Javier, and then hold the bags that were full of bird. I held my arm out and Javier looped each bag over my forearm, sliding them up. By the time we were finished both arms were held out in front of me stiffly, like a zombie, and I walked back carefully, conscious of the fluttering, the almost weightless weight, the movements like goldfish in a plastic bag at a fair.

We processed the birds strictly in order of collection. My contribution was limited to data entry – to do what Javier was doing required two different examinations and a permit. I noted down the serial number on the ring that Javier laid out ready, different-sized rings for the different-sized birds, robins got the smallest and lightest rings of all. That first song thrush didn't stop yelling for one single second. It protested as he got it out of the bag, as he measured and weighed it, screamed as Javier attached the tiny ring as quickly as he could, and all the time it was screaming it was pecking at his fingers with its strong snail-smashing beak. Javier looked lovingly, indulgently at the outraged thrush while I wrote down a zero, bird code for genderless, an 'it' because it's not possible to sex them in the winter. In the summer, apparently, it's easy because the females pull out their own breast feathers the better to warm their eggs while male birds have full breast coverage.

'Does the ring unbalance him?' I asked Javier.

'After a few days he will get used to it, it's very light.' Modern GPS trackers, he told me, offer superior technology but their cost precludes widespread adoption, and even the smallest ones are still too heavy for the lighter birds to carry.

In narrow columns I recorded the bird's age, which Javier figured out from looking at the feathers, plus its wingspan, and the length of its longest feather. I also wrote down numbers for fat and muscle mass. Javier determined this by gently blowing on the bird's abdomen and visually scoring the amount of yellow fat. He showed me how some birds are fat, hench, and winter-proofed, but some need to 'eat very soon if they're going to make it'. He could even forecast the weather from bird tummies: 'It's going to be cold in these next nights,' he proclaimed mystically, like a fortune teller. The birds had already put on more fat to protect themselves, they divine the weather before it turns, and prepare. I hoped for high mass and fat numbers, which meant the bird was robust, and I crossed my fingers that Javier wouldn't assign an F4 which meant a problem: parasites or fungal infections. F4s seemed mainly to affect the robins. Most of the robins we caught were fine but there was a very small one, dangerously underweight, who scored low across all categories and I worried for him. I drew an extra column for the song thrushes and started rating their screaming from one to five stars. That first thrush got five stars.

Trying to catch the sound of birdsong feels to me like attempting to write down the scent of perfume, impossible to render. Self-important Collins has no problem finding the words I can't, declaring that the song thrush makes 'an excited series of "electrical" scolding sounds tix-ix-ix-ix-ix… cocksure and dogmatic'. Dogmatic is the perfect word. 'They're always crying and biting,' said Javier. Unlike the hysterical song thrushes, robins never panic. Silent in their tangles, they were quietly dignified as Javier took their measurements. This tracks: robins are supposed to be able to hold the souls of dead people, so I guess it'd take more than rulers and scales to spook them. Up close their red feathers are just as cheerful as you'd hope from their christmassy reputation, and their eyes are round and glossy and alert. Collins, on the robin, says: 'curtseys and cocks [its] short tail… Call a short hard "tick", when nervous… the ticking calls are protracted… sounding like grandpa's clock being wound up'. They're also viciously territorial, males will fight to the death for a garden.

To weigh them, the birds had to go head down in one of the two sizes of plastic cups that were then put on the microscale, arse up, legs pedalling. The final indignity before Javier released them with their new ankle bracelets. To let them go, Javier laid the birds back gently on his palm. They stayed there for a few seconds staring up at the blue sky before commando rolling and spinning into flight. He worked as efficiently as possible, calling out the bird's key statistics to me in rapid fire staccato. I thought of Marilyn Monroe, 26–24–34, as I tried to keep up with him. Javier wanted them all free in the shortest possible time. In all his years of birding he'd only lost one bird in the nets – far below the average of one dead bird for every one hundred caught, and this one death only happened because an opportunistic raptor, seeing a tiny bird struggling in the net, killed it for lunch. He still thinks about it sometimes.

By now the sun was fully up and it was starting to get warmer, I was barefoot with my socks and shoes drying in a patch of sunlight. Mary Oliver said 'a poem should always have birds in it'. *The Odyssey* is full of birds, they are messengers and omens and symbols. Athena, the grey-eyed goddess, is associated with the symbol of an owl and changes into a swallow, and a sea eagle at various points in the story. Birds are used to foreshadow events and provide warnings. At one point Penelope dreams of a 'huge eagle with a pointed beak' killing twenty geese which (obviously) symbolises the impending death of all her prospective suitors. When Odysseus is lost at sea after leaving Calypso's island, the goddess Ino comes to him in the form of a gull. Birds are mystical, they have the ability to transcend worlds, moving between our mortal realm and the world of the gods. Their symbology in the story is complex, flight suggests freedom and hope, but their presence can also reveal the hand of the gods in human affairs, a shorthand for destiny and fate. Birds can tell the future.

We went back to the nets every hour. As the day lengthened, the number of birds we caught decreased. They are most active in the rising dawn. A house sparrow had somehow managed to get the net under its miniature tongue. It made me gag just watching the untangling but Javier, like a gentle surgeon, was never once flustered.

The bird's miniscule pink tongue was released unharmed. On the way back to the farmhouse for lunch, Javier, who saw everything, pointed out a tiny tortoise, the size of my thumb. Very gently he picked it up and moved it into a patch of sunlight, 'He needs to be warm.' The tortoise shell was more yellow than green. I didn't know they could come this small, this delicate.

I was allowed to release one bird. The robin lay on my palm, stunned, felt like a doll, I was barely breathing.

'When you put them on their backs and the sky is above them,' Javier said, 'it confuses them, they think they're flying.' Eventually my robin figured it out and did the same commando roll they all did, flipping over and into the air. I sent a message for him to fly back across thresholds that I couldn't see, to whisper to my father in whatever language birds use when they're not singing.

There's a hidden world of ornithologists collaborating across the globe, ringing and logging birds, gathering their data on old-fashioned clipboards with sharp pencils, entering the details into networked computers, informing each other when they find a ringed bird, interpreting the serial numbers, codes, plotting flight paths. Birds can fly thousands of miles along magnetic superhighways in the air, like it's nothing, every single year. They do extraordinary things every day, and these people are their witnesses and admirers. Their attempts to track and protect populations with swords drawn, in the face of climate change, in the teeth of despair, make me feel hopeful and worried all at once, a blended sadness.

'I have a surprise for you.' Javier smiled as he returned from the nets. I'd stayed at the desk because there weren't as many birds now and he didn't need me. It was getting on for mid-afternoon and soon all the birds would 'have a siesta' and we'd take the nets down. Slowly, with a dramatic flourish, Javier pulled out a hoopoe from the first bag. 'In Catalan,' he said, 'it's called *un pupet.*' This is the iconic bird of Menorca and for good reason: it looks like a rock star. Fairly large, just under thirty centimetres, the hoopoe's bill is long, slender and curved, it has black and white wings, and a bright orange crest. They mostly eat insects, sometimes frogs. I was allowed to hold this one for brief seconds and Javier took a photograph of us, the bird's head-feathers standing up proudly, fire-orange against the light, me grinning like a little kid.

The next bag contained a greenfinch and as Javier spread its wings they opened startlingly iridescent, bright green shading to custard yellow and softest grey. The third bag held a chaffinch which Javier said was 'a very common bird' and its fluffiness reminded me of the hatchling chicks that were born every spring at home. I looked at the elbows of its legs, the surprising sturdiness of its long claws, its dark magnetic eyes, bold and wistful all at once. Not protesting, just silently asking again to be free.

The final bag of the day held a tiny blackcap, a very small grey bird which looked like he was wearing a miniature hat. Before I saw one up close, my favourite of the tiniest birds had been the Sardinian warbler. The Sardinian is not spectacular, not showy, it's just somehow incredibly joyful as it sits in small bushes, singing of Italian islands in 'harsh, rattling verses at high speed with very brief whistled notes inserted', as Collins puts it, but my allegiance changed when I saw this blackcap. The sun was high and made it look like someone at a fashion show had painted his breast feathers gold. His round dark eyes looked straight into mine, I felt like he saw all of me, understood everything. Collins, typically, was dismissive: 'a rather stocky build... dirty grey above and light olive-grey below', but this bird was beautiful.

I got back to St Lluís in the late afternoon, muddy and tired and bird-light. The memory of feathers soft against my palm, that dry-

woody-feeling of delicate hoopoe feet curled into my fingers. Wild
birds are unreachable, untouchable, but I got to see them up close.
There are always parallel worlds. A big, busy city sharp with elbows
and lonelification and aggression, and alongside it, another world.
A world of sunlit islands where birds are taken from the sky and
released back into it. A world where you can change elements with
ease, walk from air into water, moving from gravitational pull into
sea suspension. Swim far from the shore just as rosy dawn fires up
the sky, breaking it open the same way your heart breaks for this
life and everyone inside it. An island where birds scream and soar.
I know I'll dream that night of the bright stares of magnetic-eyed
birds – the almost-nothing lightness of them, how that robin rested
just briefly, lying back against my palm for a moment, before flying
up and away.

'It was the best day for a long time,' I told Katharine on the phone.
As I talked I felt the old lightness inside me. My own plumage
colours returning, my feathers shining, just a little. I told her about
the hysterical song thrush and the dignified robin.

'You'd definitely be a song thrush,' she said.

My father was a robin.

The lightness lasted all day and into the week too. Birds came
down from the sky and brought me out from under snow. It had
been the first time I'd felt like myself again, fully absorbed, fully
in the world. As I wrote in my journal at the table in the garden,
wrapped up in a coat and scarf, I watched a robin steal pellets of
dried cat food directly from the cat's bowl, and silently applauded
him. He flicked his tail and curtseyed. He wasn't wearing a ring.

Chapter Thirteen

Portrait of an Orange

London, England

But when the brightest star that carries news
about the coming Dawn rose up the sky,
the seaborne ship neared land

I'm walking past a wall of posters for the Cezanne exhibition in London, on my way to the underground. White letters across those famous oranges, although the e has lost its accent these days. It seeps into me, this orange-ness, despite my efforts to avert my eyes, I drop them to the pavement, study the pulverised, blacked outlines of chewing gum on the dull, wet grey of the paving slabs, and wonder for the fifty millionth time why I'm living here. Even though I won't look at them directly, fat oranges sit on the edge of my subconscious all day. There's an unexpected heaviness to oranges, a heft to them.

I know what Cezanne's oranges are trying to tell me but I keep rolling them away from me. I'm avoidant. I sulk. Then I do what I always do, panic and sweat and claw at the very last minute, adrenalised, searing, wanting suddenly, like a child, but the exhibition is completely sold out. I send big-eyed emojis to friends, deploy emotional blackmail, make oblique references to last wishes, overt ones to death and its aftermath. Finally, Rachel secures a ticket somehow, because that's the kind of friend she is, but she can't come with me. There's only one left, and it's for this afternoon. I make excuses, run from work, holding a stolen umbrella against the rain. Follow the orange lamp posts and I'm there. I'm there in front of the Tate. I'm there in front of the oranges.

'With an apple, I will astonish Paris,' said Cezanne. His words printed high on the wall at the entrance to the exhibition.

Oranges and orange lamp posts.

Paul and Paul.

The painter and my father.

I cast my mind back, looking for the start.

I don't know how old I am. This could of course be cross-referenced, classified, known, but I prefer the vagueness encoded in memory, this was way back before the time of depressingly specific digital timestamps. At a guess, I would have been between ten and thirteen. I do know I was awkward and teenager-ish. I remember standing in the queue for tickets outside the Tate Gallery in London for a long while. Uncertainty mounting. Because I was alone with my father, and I was never alone with my father, ours was a classically gendered childhood – my brother went out with him on golf courses, I stayed with my mother doing whatever it was that girls did – this was never completely clear to me.

When I was a child, my father was mercurial, unpredictable, as quick to anger as he was to make a joke, he could be great fun and he could also be formidable. I found this disconcerting, and I didn't know which way today would go. His anger always came with advanced warning signs: the very slightest grinding of his jaws, a tensing of the temporomandibular muscles, the habitual air-circling of his index finger as he spoke, twirling with increasing emphasis. I wasn't exactly scared of him, I held anger in my palms too and could radiate it back when needed, equal and opposite, but I was on guard, watching carefully, the way you're supposed to train wolves never to take their eyes off you by behaving unpredictably. So far the queue didn't appear to be making him impatient and subsequently irritable, which it easily could have done. We were unused to London, to crowds, to day trips, to art, culture, galleries. My mother must have been elsewhere in the city with my younger brother.

It was just me, my father and Cezanne – who back in those days still had his é. I'd been raised in the lonely green countryside, lacking in almost every cultural pursuit, other than Brontë-worthy damp walks. This was my first trip to an art gallery. Doubly uncertain once we were inside, not sure how to behave in this space of looking. Oranges spilled across tablecloths or were contained in bowls, mixed with apples and sometimes pears. There was joy in them, that was something I knew for sure, was the extent of my art criticism, back then. My father seemed very happy, looking at the paintings. I was happy, looking with him. At him. Copying: how to peer at paintings, how to hold your arms behind your back, palm to knuckles, how to lean forward with intent. Relieved also. It seemed to be going well. He had chosen this, wanted for some reason to show me these paintings. I felt strangely grown up, his equal.

Afterwards, in the gallery shop, my father behaved oddly. My mother would have bought me something, a small, cheap thing, but something nonetheless. I asked for a poster of oranges, wanting a real memory of this strange day, but he selected a print of *The Gardener Vallier* instead, disregarding my wishes entirely. He bought himself a present. Nothing for me. This astonished me. A kind of adult behaviour I wasn't used to. Then again I never knew what to expect with him, we had spent very little time together at that age. On the train back I was empty handed, he carried a long cardboard tube. At home the print was unrolled, framed, hung. It stayed in the sitting room for the rest of his life. When he died, in that room, the print was hanging on the wall next to him.

Prints and originals. Parents and children. Perhaps that's too simplistic, reductive. Although he was original, my father. Not eccentric, but he had something I'd like to find a better word for than quirky. Character, I suppose. He was memorable, and not just to me. After he died they came to me like arrows, the memories from his friends, his patients, his colleagues. He was, of course, more than his role of father, his personhood only fully revealed to me in his absence. I collected them all, reread the letters, messages, emails. Rereading and trying to understand, I suppose, that first text that was him. A revisionist history. Originals matter. You can see details in paintings that even museum-quality prints can't convey. Details and scale.

When at last I stand in front of *The Gardener Vallier*, again, familiar and not, this particular painting is surprising. It shows a man in blue trousers and a yellow shirt sitting on a wooden chair against a dark background, but in the left corner the blue of the trousers and the yellow of the shirt is echoed, suggesting perhaps a sympathetic connection between person and landscape. Far smaller than I expected, they must have enlarged it when they manufactured the print he bought. The gardener's eyes are hidden by a low-brimmed straw hat but nevertheless, there's some kind of animation, an expectation perhaps of amusement, that I hadn't noticed before, that hadn't translated in print. And his foot too, held stiffly, at a slightly self-conscious, even theatrical, angle, and the shoe too, lighter than in the replica. It is, of course, emphatically not a painting of my father, but it is a portrait of my father that I see in it.

He sat for it too. My father, adopting the same pose, on a chair set out in my mother's freshly dug vegetable garden during lockdown. They must have brought the chair out specially. His foot is self-consciously held, pointing down. He's smiling his crooked smile and wearing a blue jumper. It flashes into me, this photograph. My brother had selected it for the back page of the order of service. I look at the original painting, feet planted, this weird magnetic pulling feeling in my legs, standing exactly in front of it, refusing to be displaced. Letting gallery people flow around me. I stare and stare. Nothing resolves itself.

I go back to the oranges at the start and look at all the different versions, trying to imagine which ones would have been in our original exhibition. Which of these paintings we would have looked at together. A nervous, long-legged girl in glasses with a clenching in her stomach, standing next to her father, proud to be with him. I curate, decide which ones would have been there and look hardest at them, trying to figure out which ones he would have liked best. A scene of a clifftop village, the Frenchness screaming out from the canvas. He loved France. I reject certain depictions of oranges and pears and apples, am drawn to others. I refuse to look at the bathing paintings at all, believing they weren't in the other exhibition. I have no evidence for any of these theories. One still life of rolling fruit catches me for long moments. I look and look. Around me babies are wheeled and narrated to, a man talks loudly and earnestly at a woman, telling her the entire backstory of Cezanne's life, giving a series of, I imagine unsolicited, observations on the arrangement of the paintings by chronology and then by theme. I move away, don't want to hear, don't want any interpretation slicing between me and the looking. I go back to *The Gardener*. Searching it. It is not a painting of my father, but it is a portrait of my father.

The deadness is the poignancy. If I just wrote, oh this painting reminded me of my dad, it would be casual, but my dead father, now that has the weight of oranges. Now he's dead, he can no longer remind me of himself, other things must. There's power in endings, in dead things, in dead things coming back to life. To haunt again, in this one, very specific way. It wasn't as though anyone else at the gallery was ghosted by my father. Just me. Ghosting with such thoughtful specificity by the dead is far more powerful than the casual workaday haunting of indiscriminate objects, things that jog memory, that stab at a thing inside you.

I called to him, and he came. Amongst the oranges and their joy. I calculate it: he died 115 years after Paul Cezanne last put down his brushes. This is how the numinous works. This is how grief works.

It holds you down but sometimes it holds you up, carries you in a rush across town to art galleries to look for ghosts in strokes of paint. It brings you orange, orange, orange.

Chapter Fourteen

Yes is a World

London and Everywhere

you really are

extraordinary

Odysseus to Penelope

It started with a boy, but it ends with me, spinning facts into story, changing narratives to suit me, just like wily old Odysseus, but isn't that exactly what a heroine should do? Shape her own text.

I miss my father in sharpness and bluntness. The sharp is sudden reminders that seize me by the throat – I burn toast and there he is holding his toast over the sink, scraping it with a knife, black crumbs everywhere. My phone ambushes me with a photograph and I'm back in Oxfordshire again, we're walking again, and I'm laughing at how he's picking his way delicately across the flooded fields, fastidiously refusing to get his shoes wet. Someone winks in a movie and my breath catches because he used to wink at me, in allyship across fraught, squabbling dining tables, in moments of hot high temper with my brother. I took an empty box of coffee filters from the house because I thought he might have touched it last. It sits on top of my mugs. I can't throw it away. Just an empty cardboard box but it falls one day into my hands when there's no reason to fall.

The blunt is more of an ache, the memory of a bruise I press my fingers into to test if it still hurts as it changes colour and lightens to almost nothing at all. I pull on his berry coloured cashmere jumper, the closest I can get to him now. To wear next to my skin the things that have warmed those I've loved is to feel connection still. Is perhaps a form of devotion, a conjuring. Here he is once more as I write. He was not the hero, not even a minor god, just another flawed character after all.

'It's too much pressure,' my father said, 'to live every day like it's your last.' He grew to hate the expression. But there are small joys, salt-water swimming and birds. Dawn, with her arms full of roses. My father wanted me to write, he kept telling me to, right up until the end.

'You have to airlift yourself out,' a friend told me when I was frozen under snow. It sounded too brutal at the time, too hard to do. I think I get it now. At least I'm learning.

'You're a big grown-up girl,' I tell Willow, my two-year-old niece who sometimes wants to be a tiny baby and sometimes wants to be a big girl. I know how she feels.

If this was a neater ending I'd tell you about the lessons I'd learned, how the journey changed me, how I'm content now in my own company, living in a house by the sea. Or how I've met the love of my life, conveniently, just as I'm writing this last chapter, and we're walking into the water holding hands, with happily ever after glinting golden on the horizon. Progressive as we think we are, there are still only two endings for a girl. The feminist one or conversely the love story. Perhaps rejecting both of these, a false dichotomy, I'll write about whatever wisdom grief contains, how I've been transformed by brushing close to death, found a way to metabolise loss, to accept, to turn it into fuel. That I live differently now, more radically, more courageously. Yes, I'll say, I ran away but now I'm running towards myself, that kind of thing. But that's not quite right either.

If I could, I would tie everything up in a bow for you, I would give you ribbons, send kingfishers skimming across the waves. I'd tell you everything's going to be okay. But the truth is far less satisfactory than a storybook adventure, life is messier than the myths. I've always been afraid of finite endings, the closing of possibility. And sometimes running is the best thing you can do.

After butchering all Penelope's suitors, Odysseus went to bed with her. They made love and afterwards:

shared another pleasure – telling stories
She told him how she suffered as she watched
the crowd of suitors ruining the house...
Odysseus told her how much he hurt
so many other people, and in turn
how much he had endured himself. She loved
to listen, and she did not fall asleep until he told it all

There's sweet intimacy in this, the long-separated couple together at last, lying in bed telling their stories, listening to each other. It's not quite the end of the poem, but this is the place I'm choosing to say goodbye to him. Our stories and how we tell them to each other matter, even Odysseus knows that. His journey humbled him, having endured 'many heartbreaking losses' he returned wiser, changed for the better. But in a way it was easy, home was a fixed place, the end of his quest was clear.

There will always be shipwrecks and storms, our heroes will die. Sometimes we're trapped on the wrong island for a long time, the maps inaccurate, the compass faulty – true north a few degrees out. Home is not always fixed, not always easy to find. Part of it, for me, is feeling connection, the people I met showed me that. I'm learning to trust my own narrative, rather than the stories and mistranslations that other people might have.

We live inside the story of ourselves, weaving our own mythologies, each life its own epic poem with deep-sea monsters and trickster gods, love and betrayal and journeys away from home. The sorrows of this world and its beauties. Its eternal beauties. I think we can choose what to pay attention to, the island or the prison in the middle of it. Everything sits alongside each other, paradise and its opposites. We can't live under enchantment our whole lives. There's pain and suffering and death but there are also those islands in between, if you know how to reach them. Those hard-won places of wonderment where time dreams, where the weather is always radiant, and where the deep blue sea wraps around you.

I know I have to put down the myths and look to the future, live inside my own stories.

New worlds open, romance and adventure call on the wind, pull through the waves, blaze the moon. I want to take off all my clothes, I want to slip into black seawater, go night swimming, feel myself move through the darkness, flip over onto my back and look up at the stars, held by the waves, held up by all of it. 'Yes is a world', a poet once wrote.

'Find the beginning' instructs the Poet to the Muse as *The Odyssey* opens. Dawn, after all, is always newborn, always rosy. We can start again. This is a love story, in a way – at least I hope it is.

I'm putting on make-up in my emerald-green bathroom, executing a perfect flick of liquid eyeliner. I don't know how this will end but I want to find out. I'm light and dizzy with want, I'm thinking maybe I really like this new boy, maybe I could hike up snowy mountains with him, but I catch myself. It's too early to tell, I don't even know him properly yet, and I've been living inside story for too long. I breathe deep and exhale long, coming back to my silvered mirror self. She looks at me, a challenge in her eyes.

There's no map for this next bit. I walk down the street, heels striking the pavement, the sound repeating me back to myself: I'm here, I'm here, I'm here. Just another girl moving across the city, towards a stranger waiting in a bar. My leather jacket makes me look tougher than I feel. I keep walking, east to west. The blue night opens into possibility, street lights haze orange, for a moment everything softens. A bike blurs past, flashing white and red, and in its wake I see a glimpse of something. I start to run, faster and faster and into the future.

Afterword

yes is a world
& in this world of
yes live
(skilfully curled)
all worlds

I wrote this book two years after my father died, as he appeared to me at the time, nearer and further away all at once. It is my version of 'a complicated man' – I didn't write him as a one-dimensional canonised saint because that would be doing him a disservice – he was far more interesting than that.

I also haven't written a lot in the book about the pandemic and it's hard to figure out how to write this section in a way that acknowledges the deep sadness of this time, our collective grief, my personal grief, my privilege, the complexity of it all, and doesn't sound defensive. I've rewritten this many times for fear of being misunderstood – I'm still not sure I've got it quite right.

This was a troubled time in the world. I was lucky to be able to travel, to be able to fund the travel with freelance work, and to make it home before my father died. Other people suffered greater losses, many could not be with their families, were not able to say goodbye to people they loved.

As mentioned in my note at the beginning, I was acutely aware of the privilege of travelling, and of the risks, both to myself and others. I worried whether I was doing the right thing, although I was fairly certain that if I returned to London I'd likely catch covid and would definitely put my health at risk in other ways. I did my best to mitigate the risks of travelling, by following the regulations of the places I visited, and observing local guidance. Almost everything in the book happened outside, including meals, people wore masks, applied hand gel, kept distance. These cautionary measures became the norm and formed the backdrop to the story. Travel was in line with the different countries' entry criteria, which was set by their respective governments' assessment of risk at the time.

We all did the best we could. Everyone struggled in the pandemic in different ways. There is, of course, no hierarchy of pain. For me, staying away from home emerged as the best thing I could do to take care of my mental and physical health at this time. As an extrovert who spins circles of people around me, I hated being stuck alone in lockdown, even as I recognise others were struggling with far bigger things. The sudden fragility of the world put into sharp focus the fact that I was alone. So the same privilege and freedom that saw me untethered from anybody or anything in London, allowing me to find some form of escape, was at the same time a great sadness. We so often want what other people have. Being with a partner and children at that time can also be seen as a kind of privilege – one that's not often acknowledged.

In another life I would have locked down with a person I loved as I worked from home. In another world my father would never have got sick, but in this reality I was met with my own limitations and the impossible fact of my father's mortality. So I left home, and in one way or another, I'm still finding my way back.

My wandering and Odysseus's journey began as an interesting parallel and gradually became something more. Odysseus longed to return home, whereas I couldn't face what was waiting for me there. But I am no scholar of ancient Greece, I've offered simplistic interpretations of the myth as a lay reader, pulling selections out of sequence from the story, to better relate them to the islands I was in. These are not chronologically ordered, nor does this book attempt to be a fully comprehensive retelling of *The Odyssey* or a survey of all the geographical theories associated with it, some of the ones I've included are deliberately lesser-known. I've sometimes described the women and goddesses in the poem as hot or sexy, to be provocative, and deliberately expose the language and limitations of the patriarchy. I'm sure there are limitations in both my reading of the myth, and in my presentation of some of the theories, for which I apologise. Any mistakes are all mine.

I hope my take on it might encourage you to read the poem and see what you can find in it. After all, it's one of the oldest adventure stories in the world and maybe it'll take you on your own journey.

Emily Wilson's sparkling translation became my guidebook and for anyone wanting to study the myth in more detail, I recommend reading her.

Parts of this have previously appeared as articles in *The Guardian* and *Condé Nast Traveller.*

Laura Coffey,
November 2023

'... *the heroes of all time have gone before us. The labyrinth is thoroughly known; we have only to follow the thread of the hero path. And where we had thought to find an abomination, we shall find a god. And where we had thought to slay another, we shall slay ourselves. And where we had thought to travel outward, we shall come to the center of our own existence. And where we had thought to be alone, we shall be with all the world.*'

Joseph Campbell

Acknowledgements

This book was a promise to my father, I didn't know at the time exactly what I was promising, or how I'd keep it. Luckily all these people helped me.

Jess Molloy, collaborating with you, not just in this book but across everything we work on together, brings joy, strengthens the work and is the best fun – it should always involve sitting on a terrace with frozen margaritas in a London heatwave. Debbie Chapman, thank you for believing in my imaginary islands, for your incredible support, for your edits that brought structure and clarity, for taking such great care with this book, and for the exquisite illustrations which make it so beautiful.

Rachel Wilkinson, for coming to find me in dark places when I was scared and alone and for bringing lamplight – you really are extraordinary.

Katharine James for keeping me (almost) sane through the pandemic, for comedy gold, for reading parts of this so many times and for your incisive edits, for CandleDaddy, for making me laugh harder than anyone.

Professor Geoffrey Hawthorn (GPH), thank you for what you taught me at Cambridge, especially on faith. I wish I could send you a copy of this book – I think of you so often. Stuart Oliver, we could not have asked for more, thank you for your beautiful care. Thank you also to 'the angels who came in the night' from Macmillan and Marie Curie. Thanks to all the Summersdale team for taking a bet on a new writer: Marianne Thompson for the sea of dreams cover, Ross Dickinson, Emma Stuart, Ben Ottridge, Jasmin Burkitt, Hannah Hargrave, Vanessa Schnall, Claire Bradley, Jess Zahra and Philippa Painter. Thank you Lisa Babalis, for riding your white pony to the rescue after a wonky read. Noah Charney. Hannah Adams. Lucy Pearson. Bonnie Galvin. Laura Barrowcliffe, Mick Hegarty and Nick Brown, thank you for your support and for trusting me with work that let me travel. Mario Rauter – bird to base, one last time. Rupert Lancaster – for your wisdom.

Thank you Jide Fadojutimi – with love. Pella Frost, for cold-water swimming in bobble hats – an addiction that has buoyed me. Alison Francis. Sue Golder. James Willliams. Izzy Coburn. Amme Poulton. Kate Scott. May Kwong. Sarah Harvey – for pink tulips and broken-ankle suppers. Simone Maini. Carrie Babcock. Thish Nadesan. The Dead Dads Club – Ros Wall, Jill Worsley, Ruth Brock. Sophie Chapman Green, Matt and Danny Green – thank you for your support, for the music. Claudia Nielsen. Billy Palmer. Mohan Mahadevan. Laura and Neal Cohen. Nick Higham. Emma Lindley. Bruce Rigal. Kat Helm – for dreamy New Court and Baker Street days. Charlie Owen. Ed Vaizey. Michael Buffham-Wade. Jane Kersel for magical realism. Marisa Levi for cover consultations and for walking water-to-water in New York City.

To my neighbours in our shared courtyard that weird spring of 2020 when I was bouncing on my trampoline, stretching on my yoga mat, and reading distractedly out in the sunshine, thank you for filling the place with flowers and keeping me company at a distance – Bev, Mo, Val and everyone else – you made London feel less lonesome and made me less afraid.

To everyone at Trailfinders who navigated with me through flight restrictions and entry requirements that kept changing, found routes and ways, remained cheerful, provided therapy as well as tickets, helped me cross borders and stay brave, even when lots of your team were on furlough. Thank you for getting me safely there and for bringing me back.

Thank you to St John's College, one of my most loved homes. Thank you Arvon and Diana Evans, James Kay and Elizabeth Jenner. Woodstock Bookshop – for encouraging me to buy Emily Wilson's translation when I hesitated. Thank you also to all independent bookshops and to all librarians. Thank you Elizabeth Taylor.

To everyone I met on this trip, thank you for telling me your stories, for opening your doors, lending me bicycles and giving me invitations, for showing me the wonderments of your islands and letting me write about them. Thank you Sonia Rocher and Liz Gireaux for the beautiful summerhouse in Menorca. Thanks and love to my Favi friends not mentioned in the book, Silvano (Lo Squalo) Cannistraro and Beppe Figliomene – for fishing, birthday celebrations and *cena*. Elisabetta Molla – for your generosity and the beach house where I could write in beauty. Viviana Filippini for the warmest, funniest friendship. Saskia Bogaarts. Fabrizio Pellegrino. Graziella and everyone at Caffè Aegusa. Maria, Daisy and Lorenzo at La Bettola – *grazie*.

Thank you to my Irish family, for storming heaven, for Christmases in Dublin and swims in December seas – Mona, Anna, Lisa, Patrick, Paul and Irish John – Paul England loved you.

Mama, for letting me write what I wanted to say, for teaching me to love stories when I was little, for teaching me to read. Patrick. Duncan and Sarah. Lucia – thank you for the beautiful calligraphy. Willow, Martha and Marlow.

Dr Paul P Coffey (PPC), I wish I could put this book into your hands. Thank you for telling me over and over to write that last year. You read the beginning of this in an early form, just a few pages emailed over, my last birthday present to you. I didn't tell you what it was, only that I was writing. You'd love that strangers are reading about you, even if you might disagree with some details, and would demand a more airbrushed, flattering portrait. The part where you made me climb a ladder up into my bedroom window remains total lunacy.

For darling Theo, littlest muse, thank you for your translations of the world, for showing me its wonders. Stay wild.

About the Author

Laura Coffey is happiest in motion. She's newly addicted to cold-water swimming, has an old addiction to adventure, and writes about the wild beauty of the places she visits and the people she meets as she roams through the world.

She has an MA and MPhil from St John's College, Cambridge University, is a certified yoga teacher and her work has been published in places like *The Guardian*, *BBC Travel* and *Condé Nast Traveller*.

When she's not writing she can be found cycling across London, stretching out on her yoga mat, hiking up a mountain, or best of all, planning an escape to a remote island.

Instagram: l_j_coffey

Copyright Acknowledgements

Excerpts from *THE ODYSSEY* by Homer, translated by Emily Wilson. Copyright © 2018 by Emily Wilson. Used by permission of W. W. Norton & Company, Inc.

Quote on page 15 from *The Glass Menagerie* by Tennessee Williams, 1944.

Quote on page 15 from *The Plague* by Albert Camus, first published in English by Hamish Hamilton, 1948.

Excerpt on page 68 from *The Group* by Lara Feigel, 2020, JM Originals (John Murray).

'Tigers' by Eliza Griswold on page 85 from *Wideawake Field* published by Farrar, Straus and Giroux, 2007.

'Ithaka' by C. P. Cavafy on page 108 from *Collected Poems* translated by Edmund Keeley and Philip Sherrard, London 1975.

'I Go Down to the Shore' by Mary Oliver on page 137 from *A Thousand Mornings* published by Corsair, 2012.

Image Credits

Cover photos by the following artists on Unsplash:
Alex Dukhanov; Benjamin L Jones; Chinigraphy; Daniel Apodaca;
Dylan Sauerwein; Giga Khurtsilava; Harry Holder;
Henrik Donnestad; Hussan Ami; Imleedh Ali Uf; James Eades;
Joyce G; Kate Sakhno; Kseniyalapteva; Linus Nylund;
Marissa Rodriguez; Mudassir Ali; Olga Pro; Pawel Czerwinski;
Resul Mentes; Sebastian Pena Lambarri; Shifaazshamoon;
Steve Johnson; Wesley Tingey; Steffi; Sime Basioli.

Other cover images © Shutterstock: Shell pattern © olgers/
Shutterstock.com; Painted brushstrokes © Fotyma/Shutterstock.
com; Sunset © Roman Kondrashov/Shutterstock.com; Pale blue
paper texture © Valery Nosko/Shutterstock.com; Island photo ©
gob_cu/Shutterstock.com; Fish and reef photo © frantisekhojdysz/
Shutterstock.com; Natural wave pattern © greoli/Shutterstock.
com; Greek wave pattern © Babich Alexander/Shutterstock.com;
Vector wave pattern © polygraphus/Shutterstock.com; Dark
blue paper texture © Charunee Yodbun/Shutterstock.com; Fish
scale pattern © best_vector/Shutterstock.com; Antique map ©
yoshi0511/Shutterstock.com; Sunrise clouds photo © Creative
Travel Projects/Shutterstock.com; Green fish © Rich Carey/
Shutterstock.com; Blue bubbles pattern © nikifiva/Shutterstock.
com; Green wave pattern © Markovka/Shutterstock.com.

Have you enjoyed this book?
If so, why not write a review on your favourite website?

If you're interested in finding out more about our books,
find us on Facebook at **Summersdale Publishers**, on
Twitter/X at **@Summersdale** and on Instagram and TikTok
at **@summersdalebooks** and get in touch.
We'd love to hear from you!

Thanks very much for buying this Summersdale book.

www.summersdale.com